AIRMEN ANON

Trevor Holman

MERLIN BOOKS LTD.
Braunton Devon

First published in Great Britain, 1992

TO
MY WIFE AND CHILDREN

ISBN 0 86303 611-2
Printed in England by Maslands Ltd., Tiverton Devon

I wish to acknowledge the wonderful help I have received from two of my colleagues — Kate Bunker and Jon Marsh. Without their constant support, enthusiasm and encouragement this booklet would never have become airborne.

Introduction

For most of my long working life I have been a technician of one sort or another. Although I am now 'retired' I am still working part-time as a school laboratory technician. Throughout these years I have met and also worked alongside hundreds of people in the field of science and technology. To my constant dismay, I have found that only a small proportion of them have had even the slightest knowledge of the duties and responsibilities of RAF ground crews during the Second World War.

This booklet is an affectionate look back at some of my RAF colleagues and our activities during those difficult years on a bomber squadron. Most of us were slightly overgrown schoolboys and schoolgirls. We were an interesting generation, having been born in the early twenties soon after the First World War and before our jobs and careers had been able to settle we suddenly realized that we were old enough to volunteer for duty in the Armed Forces, quite early on in the Second World War.

A large proportion of us came from homes that many people today would consider embarrassingly humble. They were, however, stable and caring homes. Regular correspondence took place between us and our parents and 'mail time' each morning at the guardroom provided us with a special sort of uplift and expectancy.

We had all been taught the three R's most thoroughly and many of us, including scholarship boys like myself, had School Certificate passes in several subjects including Maths and Physics which were essential to being accepted for training as Wireless/Radar Mechanics, for example. We had also enjoyed and benefited from the beautiful simplicity and tranquillity of the twenties and most of the thirties. These were precious factors that were doomed never to return. It was probably fortunate for our morale that we did not realize this as the war dragged on year after year.

How it all started

My father was an East Sussex man from the village of Ardingly, a son of the soil whose ancestors were almost certainly tilling the Sussex soil when William the Conqueror landed. My mother was a Geordie, born and bred in Newcastle. She had four brothers and a sister. One of her brothers was a fully trained and experienced engineer with Vickers-Armstrong. Just like many thousands of other men he suddenly found himself on the human scrap heap as a result of the terrible economic depression that engulfed the world from 1929 until 1939. For a few years he tried his hand at self-employed activities such as running a dairy. Eventually he had to admit defeat and, in order to remain sane, he took up wireless as a hobby, scouring the second-hand shops of Newcastle for inexpensive bits and pieces.

In August 1936 my mother took my sister and me up to Newcastle to stay with this brother. Right from the start I sat entranced, watching him winding tuning coils and transformers, then connecting them up to magical-looking components. Eventually he ended up with a wireless receiver that could pick up all the local transmissions. For me the 'wireless bug' had bitten and when our fortnight's stay came sadly to an end he generously filled a metal attaché case with precious wireless components and I brought it home to Elstree in triumph. Within a week or two my bedroom was festooned with wires all over the place and for some time my poor mother was too frightened to step into this maze for fear of causing some electrical catastrophe.

My home village of Elstree was subsequently subjected to determined bombing by the *Luftwaffe*. Mercifully, most of the two thousand assorted bombs that fell on the parish of Elstree during the blitz exploded harmlessly in the fields surrounding the village. The reason for these attacks was as follows. It had been decided round about 1938 to extend the Northern Line of the Underground from Edgware to Elstree. Work started in earnest early in 1939 and during the spring and early summer I remember cursing the non-stop drone of bulldozers working late into the night hollowing out one of the large fields to the south of the village as I swotted up in my bedroom in readiness for the School Certificate exams. Another source of dismay was the realization that this was the field that my mother, sister and I had explored in September 1926, gathering firewood from dead tree branches. The General Strike was in full swing and my parents were afraid there might not be another delivery of coal for some months. It was important to provide winter fuel for our kitchen range.

Soon after the outbreak of war in early September 1939 all this work came to a halt but the huge brick-built engine sheds were virtually complete and later in 1940 they were converted to factories for quantity production of Mosquito aircraft fuselages. The Mosquito was constructed in wood and fabric and carpenters were recruited from far and wide to man the production lines. German Intelligence obviously got wind of this early on and this is why Elstree village was 'treated' to so many night bombing attacks.

On the night of 13th February 1941 the air raid siren sounded at Elstree. My parents, sister and I rushed down to the Anderson shelter at the bottom of the garden. Very soon the anti-aircraft guns in the fields just to the north of the village opened up with a tremendous barrage. Then we heard the throbbing engines of a solitary German bomber flying over the village and heading towards London. As it passed out of range the guns ceased firing and a minute or two later we heard a tremendous explosion in the distance. It was the worst 'distant' explosion we had experienced during the four months that the night blitz had lasted thus far. This deadly bomb had been dropped on a heavily built-up area of West Hendon, between Brent Reservoir (the Welsh Harp) and the Edgware Road (the A5). Eighty-five people were killed, several hundred injured, many of them seriously, and over one thousand people were made homeless. Many theories have been put forward over the years about this bomb but I have always been convinced that it was intended to wipe out the Mosquito factory at Elstree.

Consider this. The factory was situated between the A5 that runs through Elstree and Elstree (Aldenham) Reservoir, less than a mile to the west. I have always thought that the pilot and navigator of that lone German bomber were distracted by the intense anti-aircraft barrage as they approached Elstree and over-shot the village without realizing it. Remember, German bombers had no radar aids at that early stage of the blitz. I reckon that the pilot continued to follow the A5 — it runs in a dead straight line — and after a minute or two he saw Brent Reservoir looming up, just to the west of it, and decided that this was the intended target area. By a strange quirk of fate I was to marry, in 1953, a Hendon girl who, in 1941, was a young schoolgirl living barely half a mile from that site of terrible devastation.

In October 1940, shortly after my eighteenth birthday, I volunteered as a Wireless Telegraphist in the Navy. Weeks and months went by and still nothing happened, causing me to become more and more restive. Since September 1939 I had been working as a junior clerk in an insurance company in the City. Round about April 1940 I had devised and constructed a small one-valve wireless receiver. The valve was mounted inside the tubular former of the tuning coil I had wound and was powered by two torch batteries, energizing a single, old-fashioned earpiece that I had detached from a pair of headphones. During the Dunkirk crisis in May 1940 I took this small receiver each day up to the office. At lunch-times, while my office colleagues were dashing down the stairs and out into Cheapside to buy a midday edition of one of the three London evening papers that were published in those days, I was listening intently to the BBC news bulletins on my 'personal' wireless.

One of my duties at the office was to use an elderly Addressograph machine to print addresses on envelopes each month for sending out premium reminders. I exploited this situation by stamping the morse code on one of the many blank metal plates available and thus managed to teach myself the code whilst taking shelter from daylight raids on the City and night raids back home at Elstree. I have explained why the village of Elstree was subjected to a lot of determined bombing.

Each week I bought my precious copy of *Practical Wireless*. I believe it cost about sixpence then. One morning in early April 1941, I was reading the latest copy of this magazine as I travelled up to the City. On one page there was an RAF advertisement appealing for ex-schoolboys aged 18 plus with School Certificate passes in Maths and Physics to volunteer for training as Wireless/Radar mechanics. The very next morning I went back to the Combined Recruiting Centre at Edgware, had another 'Medical' and filled in the necessary documents. We had to sign a declaration that we would be prepared to fly if required to do so. A few days later I was called to Cardington along with lots of other lads to be trade-tested, sworn in and given a number.

Before the war, Cardington, near Bedford, was the RAF's airship base. The two enormous airship hangars were still there when we arrived. All airship flights had been banned since the tragic crash of the R101 in France whilst on its long journey to India in 1931. In the spring of 1931 the R101 flew low over Elstree on one of its test flights. It was enormous and could not have been travelling at more than about forty miles per hour. As an eight-year-old boy I reckoned I could keep up with it and I sprinted excitedly along the High Street and across a huge field at the north end of the village. Eventually, of course, I collapsed exhausted in the long grass and could only watch helplessly as it drifted away northwards to Cardington. I believe Cardington's facilities were used for testing barrage balloons during the earlier years of the war.

My worst moment at Cardington came when I was seated at a small table opposite the recruiting sergeant. He had been noting down various personal details and then suddenly asked me the colour of my eyes. I was aghast, for I hadn't the slightest idea. For a fearful moment I felt sure that a firing squad would be summoned from behind a curtain and ordered to put this useless wreck of an idiot out of his misery. No such thing happened. The sergeant simply leaned across the table, aimed a piercing glance at my face and announced 'hazel' with a dropped 'h'. Almost gibbering with relief, I realized that not only had I not been exterminated but had just discovered for the first time in my young life that my eyes were ''azel'. The following morning we were sent back home and a week or two later my call-up papers arrived, ordering me to report to Blackpool. I had just completed my first week of 'square-bashing' up there when my mother wrote telling me that my Navy call-up papers had arrived and my father, very worried, had returned them with a covering letter explaining that I had now joined the RAF.

All this recent frantic activity had resulted from some superb initiative on the part of Winston Churchill. He had suddenly demanded one thousand bomber raids on Germany and was not at all pleased to be told that we did not have nearly enough technicians to service this number of bombers together with their equipment, quite apart from any overseas expansion that might be needed by the RAF. He immediately set in motion what was to become a brilliantly successful technical training programme.

The Wireless/Radar Mechanic Course

We had been at Blackpool for barely a fortnight when, on the second Friday there, we were told in the morning that we were going to the firing range to be trained in the use of Lee-Enfield rifles. We were somewhat stunned by this information for we had been under the impression that our basic training at Blackpool would last for four weeks. Anyway, we spent several rather nervous hours at the firing range that day. It was difficult to adjust to the 'kick-back' of the Lee-Enfield rifle but in the end we managed it. We discovered, much later, that this curtailment of our basic training was due to Winston Churchill who had been fretting and fuming over the delay in getting us on to our technical training courses, declaring that the RAF was in urgent need of technicians, not soldiers. The following day we assembled at Blackpool Central Station and found ourselves on a train heading south. There was much joy among those of us who came from the London area. This joy was short-lived, however, for when the train arrived at an isolated siding there was a lengthy pause during which another engine was hitched on to the rear of the train and we found ourselves travelling northwards. We ended up at Heysham harbour and embarked on a troop-ship that was bound for Belfast. We were put through life-belt drill because of the constant threat of U-boat attacks. This was July 1941 and most of us had very little sleep that night. We were excited but also anxious, realizing that our parents had no knowledge of what was happening to us. I and lots of the other lads were up on deck as dawn broke about 4.30 a.m. I shall never forget the magical first sighting of the Emerald Isle with its incredible green slopes sweeping down to the sea. The first part of our Wireless/Radar Mechanic course was to take place at Belfast College of Technology. We were billeted at the Presbyterian Hostel in Belfast. Thus began the tranquil academic life that I had hoped to achieve at Oxford or Cambridge via a scholarship from school before the outbreak of World War II crushed my dreams. We were assigned to the barrage balloon squadron protecting Belfast from low-level air attacks. I revelled in the splendid bookshops and second-hand markets of Belfast which were still existing in a sort of time-warp in spite of some heavy air raids earlier on. The local people were wonderfully hospitable and we received many invitations to their homes. It ended up with some of us escorting their daughters, in a very proper and 'English' manner, up to Cave Hill on the outskirts of Belfast for weekend afternoon picnics. On Saturday mornings, after our weekly drill session, we used to make a tour of the sweet shops. Sweets were not yet rationed in Belfast but were in short supply and had largely disappeared under the counter. We used to 'chat up' the girl assistants and usually managed to come away with a few bars of coveted chocolate. I began to experience an inner feeling that these idyllic conditions could not last much longer for me. Everything was too perfect to be true.

Close by the college there was an excellent YMCA canteen that sold home-made cakes. Lined up on the counter, costing one penny each, were half-pint bottles of rich, creamy milk. Each bottle had the usual waxed cardboard disc pressed into its neck. There was also a push-through inner ring in each disc for the insertion of a drinking straw. As a child I never drank cold milk, much to the distress of my mother, but after experiencing months of harsh rationing back home the sight of this rich milk got the better of me and I began to indulge each morning at break-time. I had been on the course for about four weeks when I became aware of a persistent stiff neck and noticed a swelling under the right-hand corner of my jaw-bone. I had never had a serious illness in my life and at first I shrugged it off as a passing nuisance. After a few days, however, the size of the swelling under my jaw-bone had increased ominously and I decided to report to sick quarters. The medical officer was a middle-aged, quietly spoken Ulsterman with kindly grey eyes. He examined me and seemed to be perplexed and worried. He immediately arranged for me to be admitted to the military hospital on the outskirts of Belfast. It was a large red-brick building and I believe it had originally been the headquarters of an Officers' Training Unit before the war. The surgeon (who was one of the King's surgeons) examined me and, like our medical officer, appeared to be perplexed. After the lapse of a week he told me that he had a shrewd idea of the cause of the trouble and explained that initially he would remove the 'rogue' gland in the side of my neck that was causing the infection. His earlier examinations had revealed that glands half-way down my back were enlarged. Each Tuesday was normally 'butcher day' at the hospital and I was made ready for my first operation. That Tuesday I waited and waited, watching with increasing envy as most of the other lads in the ward enjoyed their breakfast, lunch and then tea. It was about 6.30 p.m. when I was finally taken down to the operating theatre. Being August, there was bright sunlight streaming in through the windows of the operating theatre — remember, it was a 'converted' hospital. I was placed on my left side on the operating table and a white linen cloth was arranged over my face. A local anaesthetic was injected into the side of my neck and the operation began. Shortly afterwards I became aware of some urgent, agitated sounds. Glancing up at the linen cloth I could see a pool of blood lying in a small hollow in the cloth just above my right eye.

"Are you feeling OK?" a voice called out.

"Yes!" I replied lustily, although I couldn't help wondering why I had been asked that question and why there was a pool of blood on top of the linen cloth. A few minutes later the cloth was removed carefully from my face and I was taken back up to the ward. About three weeks later I was prepared for my second operation — the removal and cleaning out of the huge internal abscess that had been steadily forming under the corner of my jaw-bone. I think I should explain at this point that our armed forces in Ulster took part in frequent manoeuvres and whenever these occurred it was almost as if a separate war had broken out, for serious casualties came streaming into the hospital inundating the surgeon with lots of urgent work.

Naturally, I had been more than curious to discover what was wrong with me. One morning, just before the surgeon was due to come round the ward I managed to scramble to the foot of the bed and take a quick look at my notes. The surgeon had queried the possibility of several ghastly diseases. My morale sank to a new low. Unfortunately, I didn't have time to scan through all his notes.

The Army ward orderly was a diligent, efficient type of chap but also somewhat sadistic — a sort of rough diamond. The day before my second operation was due he came along to my bed to have a chat.

"You nearly snuffed it the other evening, mate," he said, with immense relish and went on to describe how the surgeon, who had been operating all that day with virtually no break, had accidentally 'nicked' my jugular vein in the process of removing the infected gland in my neck. "Luckily," the orderly continued, "he managed to clip and stitch your jugular just in time — there was blood everywhere!" By now he was almost drooling at the mouth but I just chuckled to myself.

The following morning I managed to read the remainder of the surgeon's notes and discovered that my 'trouble' was bovine tuberculosis, caused by drinking milk from cows infected with this disease. This explained why my first operation had been the final one of the day. The surgeon had obviously not wished to risk contaminating the operating theatre with other operations to follow. I was taken down to the operating theatre about mid-afternoon. Ether was the anaesthetic used in those days. It was very effective but made one feel terribly sick for some time after regaining consciousness. The nurses, who came from one of our leading London teaching hospitals were magnificent. I discovered that my head was surrounded by small, clinical sandbags to prevent excessive movement. With the infected gland and the abscess now removed my rate of recovery increased considerably.

Occupying a bed in the corner of the ward — just two beds away from me — was a young Canadian soldier. He had been on a troop-ship bound for Ulster and just a few miles out from the Ulster coastline his ship had been torpedoed by a German U-boat. His left leg had been badly shattered and he had to undergo bone-graft after bone-graft. His only sighting of the British Isles had been this military hospital in Belfast. Once a week his left leg had to be gently manipulated in order to find out how much progress had been made. His screams of agony and desperate pleas for the manipulation to stop have haunted me to this day. I had many a long chat with him and felt terribly guilty when finally discharged from hospital, leaving him to face up to more operations on his left leg.

I remember stumbling out through the open gates of the hospital and into the early evening noise and bustle of Belfast's traffic. It was now late November 1941 and for the past eleven weeks I had been hidden away in a ward of a military hospital in large secluded grounds. The outside world suddenly seemed terribly noisy and bewildering. I think I should mention now that we were able to purchase from the squadron's flight sergeant, a cheery, canny old Scot, small blue bakelite discs about the size of the old halfpenny at a penny each. One of these discs entitled us to travel to the terminus of any tram route apart from the Falls Road ares. The RAF certainly looked after us young lads. I arrived at the Presbyterian Hostel just in time for tea, to be greeted with friendship and good wishes from my colleagues who were now approaching the end of the first part of the course and bracing themselves for the final exam.

The following morning I reported to the squadron office to receive a travel warrant for my fortnight of sick leave together with strict instructions to report back to the medical officer immediately upon my return. Five months had elapsed since I joined the RAF and it was good to be going back home although the circumstances were somewhat regrettable. The boat journey from Larne to Stranraer followed by the long overnight rail journey to Euston seemed endless, but at last I made it. My parents were delighted to see how well and fit I looked. They had expected to see me looking thin and gaunt. In what seemed no time at all my sick leave came to an end and I found myself at the start of the long journey back to Belfast. I reported to the squadron office and then made my way to the medical officer. I thought he looked somewhat sad as he beckoned me into his consulting room. Coming straight to the point he informed me gently and quietly that I was to be discharged from the RAF on medical grounds. For a few moments my head swam and all I could think of was the feeling of shame and disgrace that my parents would experience. I pulled myself together, realizing that I had a tough struggle on my hands. I quietly pointed out to him that I had never felt fitter and had represented my school at cricket, Rugby and athletics. I was desperate, for I had been to considerable lengths to join up in the first place. I pleaded, argued, threatened and cajoled. The medical officer listened in polite silence and finally, realizing that I was genuinely anxious to stay in the RAF, he said he would see what he could do and asked me to call round the following morning. I was there like a shot from a gun. There was no further development to report but he asked me if I would care to wire up an extension loudspeaker in one of the bedrooms upstairs to the wireless set downstairs.

This was one of those beautiful pre-war Murphy wireless receivers in a superb polished cabinet and had a huge tuning dial that spanned the whole world of broadcasting. I set to work delightedly, carefully routing the wires behind the picture rail downstairs and then unobtrusively up to the bedroom. I doubt if I have ever worked so carefully and with so much attention to detail as I put into this task. When completed, the extension loudspeaker was tested and it functioned splendidly. The medical officer declared himself to be well satisfied and asked me to report back the following morning. Years later, looking back on this event I realized that he had decided to put me to a practical test to see if I was worthy of any efforts on his part to ensure that I stayed in the RAF. I reported back the following morning and I had a vague sort of feeling that his Irish eyes were smiling ever so slightly as he called me into his room. He told me that I was to be downgraded to Grade 3 for medical reasons, but I could stay on in the RAF and rejoin the training course at the college. I almost fell on his neck in gratitude.

It was now mid-December 1941 and a large contingent of American GIs had recently arrived in Ulster. Their medical officers checked and tested the quality of the milk and rejected it out of hand, sending back urgent requests to America for supplies of milk. This enraged the Ulster farmers who, naturally enough, had been looking forward to rich pickings from supplying dairy produce to a large number of American troops.

In fairness to the RAF I feel I should mention that I discovered, much later, our medical profession in 1941 had very little knowledge of bovine tuberculosis and the RAF, in its wisdom, decided to discharge me rather than have an 'unknown quantity' on its hands.

I was assigned to a class at the college at a stage of the course that I had reached when I went into hospital and life returned to normal. During the weeks that followed I formed a strong friendship with a Scottish lad called Jimmy. His father ran a wireless and electrical business in Dundas Street, Edinburgh. Throughout the previous year or two Jimmy had assisted his father in the shop during school holidays, learning to repair wireless receivers. In this way he had become very experienced and as wireless had been my hobby for several years I revelled in having such a knowledgeable friend. The remaining weeks of the course sped by and then came the final exam which was excellent.

Afterwards, Jimmy and I were called to the RAF officer in charge of the training course. He told us we were to take our week's leave and then report back to the college to commence a six months' stint as Instructors. We were not asked if we would like to 'have a bash' or if we thought we could cope. There was a world war of technology raging about our heads. The number of trainees arriving at the college had been increasing steadily and the college had become seriously short of instructors. Jimmy and I made our way back to the hostel in a sort of daze.

Upon our return to Belfast we immediately prepared to take up our new duties. I must admit I was feeling a bit apprehensive, especially when I discovered that two of the 'pupils' in one of the new classes were maths masters who had been called up recently when the age limit for reserved occupations was raised to cater for the rapidly increasing demands of the armed services. Jimmy and I were only nineteen years old but we quickly settled down to our new environment. I had felt a bit worried about Jimmy because he was a sensitive, quietly spoken young Scotsman whose mother had died suddenly and unexpectedly a few weeks earlier. I had been assigned the task of accompanying him to the railway station and seeing him off on his brief but sad return home to Edinburgh for his mother's funeral. However, we both ended up enjoying this new experience of helping other airmen to master a difficult and somewhat abstract subject.

The weeks passed by happily enough but I suddenly realized that, with the war breaking out just three weeks before my seventeenth birthday, I had not had the opportunity to learn ballroom dancing, still the most popular pastime in 1942. I decided to correct this situation and one evening I made my way to Albert White's ballroom where they held instruction classes for beginners. I paced up and down outside the entrance for some time before plucking up sufficient courage to go in through the door and up a long flight of stairs. Wearing a somewhat ill-fitting uniform with trousers that were a shade too long didn't exactly boost one's morale. The lady instructors were superb. They put one at ease immediately and within minutes I was exploring the intricacies of the slow foxtrot.

The weeks passed quickly and our six months' stint as instructors was drawing to a close. Jimmy and I were due to go on the Radar Mechanic course at Malvern along with the 'upper crust' of those about to take their final exam. We had been looking forward to this because although radar was on the secret list we had heard some whispers about the extraordinary new techniques in electronics that had already evolved. However, a day or two before the course ended we were called once again to the officer-in-charge. He explained that he had just received an urgent message from Bolton College of Technology where the training course for Wireless Mechanics was taking place. They were becoming seriously short of instructors and therefore Jimmy and I would report to Bolton after our week's leave, take the Wireless Mechanic course and then stay on as instructors. There was a war on and it would have been pointless for us to say that we were more than entitled to go to Malvern on the Radar Mechanic course. We took our week's leave and duly reported back to Bolton.

The Wireless Mechanic Course

I found myself billeted at an off-licence at a sort of 'village' about a mile from Bolton along the road to Bury. The landlord was a small, quiet man — the living image of Emlyn Williams, the famous Welsh actor and playwright. His wife was a large, formidable woman with huge forearms like hams and a scourging tongue. Whenever he wanted a drink he nipped over the road to the pub opposite. At first I thought it odd that, with the shelves of the off-licence crammed with bottles of beer and stout (no canned beer then), he had to pop over the road. I quickly discovered the reason for this habit of his. He soon regarded me as an ally and invited me to accompany him 'over the road' before lunch each Sunday. For my sins I was introduced to Lancashire Stout. During each of the two world wars the government of the day decreed that the gravity of beer would be reduced for the duration. This was to reduce the risk of accidents to munitions workers and maintain the required rate of output. This stout, however, was real 'stingo' to me. We used to nip back over the road just before Sunday lunch was due, feeling rather sheepish. His wife would be standing just outside the street door, her huge arms folded menacingly and her beady eyes surveying us with darkest suspicion. We used to sidle past her and sit meekly and innocently at the dinner table. They had a daughter, a somewhat thin, unhealthy-looking girl who was in the ATS — the army equivalent of the WAAFS and WRENS. For some reason she seemed forever to be trying to trap me in a corner of the parlour. I always felt much safer with an honest glass of stout in my hand on Sundays.

The Lancashire folk, just like those in Belfast, were wonderfully hospitable, homely and cheerful and, of course, they spoke with that delightful Lancashire accent. I greatly admired the fortitude of the girls, most of them working in the local spinning mills. They used to walk along cheerily and jauntily with cold winds and rain beating down on them, causing their bare legs to become almost blue with cold. Clothing coupons were few and far between and stockings had to be placed well down the list of requirements. There was an excellent Palais de Danse at Bolton and from time to time I was able to put into practice the ballroom dancing skills I had acquired in Belfast.

I feel it is time to concentrate on the Wireless Mechanic course. It was a very intensive one and we had lots of homework to do each evening. In one of the large workshops at the college they had installed the fuselage of a Wellington (Wimpey) bomber. We were taught all our practical skills on this fuselage. It was a great thrill for us to learn that this particular aircraft had done its stint of war service. For the practical part of our final exam the instructors inserted deliberate faults into the equipment and installations and, taking turns, we had to detect and correct as many of these faults as possible. It was superb training for our forthcoming duties on a squadron.

During the war this country observed continuous double summer time and one particular memory of Bolton that stands out is that when September 1942 arrived it was pitch dark as we assembled outside the college at 8 o'clock each morning for roll-call. I need hardly add that before Jimmy and I had completed the course the college had acquired sufficient instructors and we simply ended up as Wireless Mechanics. We could, of course, have remustered and gone to Malvern on the Radar Mechanics course but we both felt the call of the open air. We had been involved with our excellent Technical Training Command for a long time but wanted to get on to a squadron.

On a Squadron

It is important to know right from the start that over ninety per cent of the servicing of the bombers had to be carried out in the open air. This meant that in hot summer weather the bombers were like tropical incubators, the perspex 'roofs' of the cabins and gun turrets focusing the sun's rays like magnifying lenses. In cold winter weather, of course, they were like refrigerators. Needless to say, my introduction to squadron work with Halifaxes occurred during the cold winter of 1942/43.

The first thing I discovered was that in extra cold weather most of the mid-upper gunners on our squadron seemed to acquire a manic ability to shoot down the external aerial that was connected to the Wireless Operator's transmitter and receiver. He, in turn, had to let out his trailing aerial to take its place. All this was baffling at first but, as we shivering, frozen-fingered wireless mechanics struggled to repair and re-erect the aerials that were suspended between a fixture on top of the fuselage and one of the tail fins, the penny finally dropped. We had been trained to leave a reasonable amount of slack in the wire when erecting these aerials. We suddenly realized that when the air temperature was very low, especially when our bombers were flying at about 20,000 feet, the stainless steel strands of the aerial wire contracted considerably. This removed the slack in the aerial, causing it to become taut as it moved upwards, bringing it right in line with the guns of the mid-upper turret.

I shall always remember with affection the attitude of our mid-upper gunners towards these incidents over which they had no control. They were always most concerned and apologetic. Incidentally, we experienced exactly the same aerial problem in cold weather, some months later, when we had to change over suddenly from Halifaxes to Lancasters, but more about that later on. I feel I should mention at this stage that we worshipped the very ground our aircrews trod. They were our gods and rightly so. Whenever one or more of our aircraft failed to return from an op we all experienced a deep sense of personal loss. Mercifully, the losses on our Pathfinder squadron were relatively small.

Pats of butter

Wartime bread was called the National Loaf. It was an excellent bread, half-way between brown and white. Teatime was an important occasion each day. We made our way (duties permitting) to the cookhouse from an aerodrome that was often cold and windswept. There was a plentiful supply of bread, including lots of spare slices, stacked in a large wooden tea chest placed on the floor at the far end of the serving counter. The problem was that an extra slice of bread was of little use if one didn't have any extra butter to spread on it. Each slice of bread on the serving counter (we were allowed to take only one of these) had a pat of butter nestling on it. As we filed past the counter the cookhouse sergeant, a huge would-be bully of a man, stood with hands on hips glowering first at us and then at the pats of butter. "They are all the same!" he snarled every few seconds. But, of course, they were not all the same. Those pats had been cut by a hurried, harassed hand. Some of them were a good fifteen per cent larger than others. The vital technique was to make our scooping up of a slice appear as random and casual as possible. Some of us were better at this deception than others. As we approached the counter it was important to pin-point at least four of the larger pats of butter in case the three lads in front happened to select three of these coveted items. No computer has ever operated more rapidly or accurately than our eyes and brains at teatime.

Take-off duty

Our squadron consisted of three flights, A, B and C, and each flight comprised eight bombers. One member of each trade was detailed to report to his own main flight dispersal hut an hour before take-off. The purpose of this exercise was to attend to and correct any late faults that occurred. It was always a tense and nerve-racking experience and as the aircrews arrived and the engines started to rev up we stood there with all fingers crossed. There was a complete black-out imposed on the aerodrome after dark. The only light permitted was the small signalling lamp operated from the take-off caravan situated at the side of the starting point of the runway. A quick flash from this lamp indicated to the next aircraft that it was all clear to take off.

I was on take-off duty on a particularly cold, black night. Everything went smoothly without a single hitch on our flight and the other two flights appeared to have experienced a trouble-free take-off. Our Flight Sergeant was delighted and told us to jump into the back of the flight lorry so that he could drive us round the aerodrome perimeter to the canteen. Shivering but elated, we quickly jumped into the lorry. We hadn't been travelling for more than a few seconds when we suddenly swerved violently to the right, sending us sprawling into the front left-hand corner of the lorry which then ground to a halt. In a semi-dazed condition we wondered what on earth could have happened. It transpired that one of the bombers on C flight, at the opposite end of the aerodrome had developed some last-minute engine trouble. This had been corrected within a short space of time but had led, of course, to the mistaken belief that all our bombers had taken off. It resulted in this particular bomber taxiing straight towards us on the perimeter track as it came round to the runway for take-off. When you realize that each bomber was painted black on the underside and dark brown and green camouflage pattern on the upper side it was a miracle of good fortune that our sergeant driver spotted it just in time. If we had collided with the bomber the lorry could have crunched straight into the bomb-bay detonating the entire bomb load of the Halifax. This would have been a major tragedy and 'yours truly' would not be writing now if this had happened.

During the summer months, take-off was carefully timed to ensure that it would be dark as our bombers crossed the enemy coastline. The whole scene was totally different. Instead of darkness enveloping the bombers and personnel, everything and everyone were exposed in broad daylight. The situation was just as tense as in winter, but as we watched our bombers take off and set course for the Continent with the sunset behind them, we felt terribly helpless, thinking back feverishly over the day's activities, hoping against hope that our inspection and testing had not missed out on any vital detail. With the war grinding on for seven days each week it was difficult to ensure that monotony and repetition were not allowed to 'dilute' constant vigilance and accurate observation. It was important to maintain continual self-criticism and self-checking.

On a lighter note, I shall always remember one particular take-off episode in late summer 1943. The temperature had been in the eighties all through the day but the bombers had been prepared carefully and we went in for tea feeling hot and tired but quietly satisfied. Later on, a number of us went round to the NAAFI canteen for a quiet coffee and chat before making our way over to our dispersal huts ready for take-off. To our amazement, there, on the canteen counter was a small barrel of cider. It was the first time that most of us had seen such a thing. Luckily, the majority of us were fairly broke as it was rather late on in the week. However, quite a number of the lads, normally teetotal, began to indulge, regarding the cider as a very attractive thirst-quencher as the evening was still very hot. The rest of us quickly became alarmed as the cider began to take its toll, for there would have been hell to pay if any of our aircraft had failed to take off because of ground crews who had become immobilized by cider. We hurried back to our living quarters to round up as many of our colleagues as possible, frantically explaining the situation. There was a concerted rush out to the dispersal huts. Several of us shared duties to which we were not accustomed but mercifully all our aircraft took off smoothly without a hitch and there was no pack drill for anyone.

I mentioned just now that most of us were fairly broke and perhaps this is a suitable point to explain that the pay of an ordinary airman was 2/6d ($12\frac{1}{2}$p) per day (Group 1 Trade, the highest paid trade), paid weekly. Out of this, most of us made a voluntary allotment to our homes of 1/- (5p) per day. This ensured that in the event of our being killed while on active service our families would receive a pension of 7/- per week. These figures may seem paltry now, but when I point out that my father's pay, as a brilliant gardener, was just two pounds per week it may help to put things into perspective.

'Stand-down'

At infrequent intervals the squadron was granted a stand-down. This meant that the squadron, as a whole, was rested for twenty-four hours and as these concessions occurred mainly during the late autumn and winter months we knew that we were in for a twenty-four hour period of non-stop heavy rain and low cloud that would make flying unnecessarily hazardous.

From 1941 onwards it was virtually impossible to buy batteries for cycle lamps and torches, especially if you lived and worked in the middle of nowhere. Apart from the fortnightly liberty bus from camp to Cambridge which was usually fully booked well in advance anyway, our only means of transport were our bicycles which we had brought from home by train at the earliest opportunity after discovering the enormity of the geography and isolation of a bomber aerodrome.

The police of the local villages, who always seemed to know exactly what went on at our aerodrome, were well aware of the fact that when we were granted a stand-down there would always be a group of us who would be mad enough to cycle the fifteen miles or so into Cambridge in torrential rain and then back to camp. This meant that we would be making the return journey after dark without lights on our bicycles. This was not as dangerous to other traffic as might appear at first because, due to severe petrol rationing, there was very little traffic on the roads. We knew from previous experience that the police would wait in ambush just to the east of Toseland crossroads. With the rain still beating down we used to set off grimly along the main road (indeed, the only road) leading back to Graveley. Then, when a mere hundred yards or so short of Toseland we veered off suddenly to the left, crashing through a spinney and then out into an open ploughed field squelching with mud. By now the local constabulary were in hot pursuit, their fully functional cycle lamps betraying their position. Urging our tired young muscles into a final exhilarating burst of energy we skidded and squelched our way in a wide arc back on to the road and then safely back to camp. I never did hear of any of my colleagues being caught and I always had the impression that the local police looked upon these encounters as a sort of friendly rivalry and something that helped to liven up what would otherwise have been a terribly drab winter evening. I often wondered why some of us felt the need, on these occasions, to go flogging into Cambridge in pouring rain, especially as we had very little money to spend. Perhaps it was because we simply wanted to get to the nearest conglomeration of buildings and people after the relative loneliness and isolation of the wide open spaces of the aerodrome.

Bomb armourers and bomb winches

I was always fascinated by the skills and techniques of the bomb armourers. At the start of bombing-up a tractor hauled a large trolley of assorted bombs up to the front of the aircraft and then a couple of armourers took over, manoeuvring the heavy trolley into position under the bomb bay. This required considerable muscle power and skill. It was certainly more difficult than appeared at first sight. An armourer, carrying a hand winch, leapt in through the entrance hatch and made his way up to the front half of the aircraft. The flat floor above the bomb bay had a number of narrow slots running fore and aft. He lowered the hook, attached to the steel cable of the winch, down through the appropriate slot to the armourer waiting below who engaged the hook with the ring fitted to the bomb. This was the real skill, the armourer up above always selecting the correct slot and the armourer down below always having the trolley in the correct position ready for the next bomb. From time to time the bomb load was changed at the last minute after the initial bombing-up. Either there had to be more target indicators and fewer high explosives or vice versa. We never knew if this was due to a late change in the weather or to the actual target.

One of the armourers, who came from Hull, was a burly and vociferous type of chap but was also the salt of the earth. On these occasions he swore and cursed non-stop for fully five minutes at each aircraft as he worked swiftly and accurately. He then proceeded to describe in vivid and explicit detail exactly what he was going to do to Hitler when he finally laid hands on him. I often marvelled that the undercarriages of the huge bombers didn't just crumple and collapse under these verbal onslaughts.

Another armourer was cast in a much gentler mould. He was a concert pianist and continually fretted and worried about the state of his hands. His name was Cyril and he was quite convinced that he would never be able to play the piano competently again, although he entertained us well enough on the canteen piano. One afternoon, bombing-up was in full swing. One of the bombs on each aircraft was to be a 4,000 lb. 'cookie' and this is when poor old Cyril came to grief. He was helping to bomb-up one of the aircraft but failed to engage correctly the ring on the 'cookie' with the release hook on the carrier. The net result was that the 4,000 lb. bomb fell a good eight feet from the bomb bay down on to the reinforced concrete of the dispersal pan, lying there in a twisted, somewhat distorted state. The grapevine went into action immediately and several of us cycled round to the far side of the aerodrome to survey the scene. Armourers from the bomb dump were hurriedly called over to inspect the bomb. After a few minutes they pronounced it safe and serviceable but before it could be winched up again some wag had chalked 'Cyril's Folly' on it.

In late 1943 the hand-wound bomb winches used by the armourers were replaced with hydraulic winches that were activated by an oil that was almost colourless. Possibly this change resulted from a realization that D-Day was approaching and it might well be important from then on to speed up the process of bombing-up. Anyway, for the wireless and radar mechanics at least, this changeover presented new problems and difficulties. The transmitters, receivers and indicators, etc. that were installed and serviced were large and heavy. It seemed to us that we were forever struggling back and forth through the fuselage of the bombers carrying a heavy piece of expensive equipment. We did not dare drop, knock or damage these heavy items. However, with the coming of the hydraulic winches our days were turned into something approaching a nightmare. You see, whenever oil was used in a hydraulic system in those days you inevitably experienced leakage and seepage. The net result was, for us, that a thin but dangerous film of colourless oil spread across the shiny, well-worn metal floor of each aircraft. As we carried our heavy burdens to and fro we often began to slip and slide, our bodies contorting rather like a Charlie Chaplin burlesque. Not daring to drop or damage our precious cargo our heads, shoulders, elbows, knees and ankles often buffeted against the sharp ribbing and fixtures of the aircraft fuselage to ensure a safe passage for this expensive equipment. I still get an occasional twinge in my left elbow, especially when there is an R in the month, but it is merely a cherished reminder of those hectic days of youthful effort and endeavour back in the early forties.

With Bomber Command handling thousands of bombs each week I suppose it was inevitable that there would be a tragic accident involving bombs from time to time. One of these accidents occurred on our squadron in the late summer of 1944 just as pay parade was about to commence one Friday morning. The procedure for pay parade was as follows: One of the hangars was cleared of aircraft and equipment and a trestle table was set up near the entrance with neat piles of 'silver' coins and ten-shilling notes. We 'ordinary' airmen stood to attention in the hangar as the Pay Officer arrived and seated himself at the table. He proceeded to call out the first airman's name, who responded by calling out the last three digits of his RAF service number, marched briskly up to the table, saluted and received his pay.

On this particular morning the Pay Officer was just about to call out the first name when there was a tremendous explosion and blast that almost knocked us off our feet. The ten-shilling notes went fluttering up into the air and wafted all over the hangar. For a few moments there was a stunned silence as we all realized instantly that a terrible tragedy had just befallen our squadron. Then, quietly and dutifully, we all began to pick up the notes and returned them to the table. There wasn't the slightest attempt at any trickery and pay parade proceeded as normal. It transpired that the explosion took place in the bomb dump that was situated in a field about two and a half miles away from the hangar, just outside the perimeter of the aerodrome. We never did hear how many armourers had been killed in the explosion, but of course the bomb dump armourers were back-room boys whom we were rarely able to meet and get to know.

One evening, a few weeks after this incident, we were on take-off duty. Everything appeared to be going smoothly when we heard and felt a tremendous explosion in the distance. Instinctively, we felt that this could be another RAF tragedy and our worst fears were confirmed a day or two later. The explosion had occurred at take-off at RAF Wyton aerodrome which was about six miles north of Graveley as the bomber flies. One of their Lancasters was taxiing round the perimeter track ready for take-off when the entire bomb-load exploded. As RAF Wyton was another Pathfinder squadron their take-off time, naturally, was synchronized with ours and this is how we came to hear and feel this tragic explosion.

For some time I was puzzled as to why, after bombing-up, the doors of the bomb bays were always left open until the final moment before the bombers started to taxi round the perimeter for take-off. This procedure caused us some anxious moments, especially from June 1944 onwards as I shall explain later. I realized, after some time, that this procedure had been adopted in case there happened to be a last-minute change in the composition of the bomb load of each aircraft. In this event it saved precious time to have the bomb doors already open.

Sundays

The war went on for seven days a week and the only event that distinguished Sunday from any other day was the arrival, at lunch-time, of a battered open car from the nearby village of Offord, crammed with Sunday newspapers. As we queued up outside the cookhouse for lunch we each purchased a newspaper. My favourite at that time was the *Sunday Dispatch* which, I'm afraid, disappeared without trace soon after the war. I was always most impressed with the quiet efficiency by which the daily papers appeared on sale in the guardroom each morning. In those days I bought my beloved *News Chronicle* and continued to do so until sadly it was cut off in its prime in the early sixties. Wartime newspapers, of course, were restricted to just a few pages because of newsprint rationing but those papers were read by young people with a thoroughness and avidity that I have rarely witnessed again for several decades now.

Flying at last

I doubt if it has ever been generally known that some of us on ground crew duties were called upon occasionally to fly with a particular aircrew on a test flight. This was usually a sudden arrangement, occurring just as we were about to begin our morning round of daily inspections of the aircraft following the previous night's op. From time to time an aircraft would develop some trouble with either its intercom or some other piece of equipment whilst it was in flight. Everything returned to normal once the aircraft was back on the ground. There was nothing for it but to grab a test meter from the dispersal hut, a few hand tools, hop into the aircraft (without a parachute) and away on a test flight. It is important to point out that the aerodrome was roughly two miles in diameter. It would have taken about half an hour to cycle half-way round the perimeter track to the parachute section, get kitted out with a parachute and cycle back to the aircraft. There just wasn't that sort of time to spare on a wartime bomber squadron.

There were more thrills ahead when we made occasional flights in our latest Mark III Halifaxes. These were magnificent aircraft and could climb, without a bomb load, almost like a Spitfire, or so it seemed to our stomachs. It was extremely rewarding to have these occasional opportunities to fly alongside some of our revered aircrews.

Keep the home fires burning

Before I recount this next episode and the wrath and indignation of anyone reading it come crashing down on me, there is one important geographical feature of our aerodrome that I must point out. It was situated little more than thirty miles south of The Wash. This meant that between us and Siberia there was only low-lying land and whenever a freezing east wind set in it would come screaming across Europe, completely unhindered and scythe its way across our aerodrome. Our Nissen huts had a concrete floor and semi-circular corrugated iron surround that formed a combined roof and walls. This form of construction turned them into refrigerators in cold weather.

It was a typical 'Siberian' night in early 1943. Several of us had been on take-off duty and although everything had gone smoothly we returned to our Nissen hut hoping to find some warmth and comfort. To our dismay we discovered that there was no coal left for the tall, cylindrical stove with chimney pipe going up and out through the roof. We immediately held a council of war and decided that six of us should raid the coal dump within the boundary of the aerodrome. This would entail crawling noiselessly beneath the lighted windows of the guardroom. We decided against the use of paper bags for the coal as the paper would make a rustling noise and possibly give the game away. As plastic bags had not yet been invented there was nothing for it but to shove the lumps of coal straight into our coat pockets. The operation was a complete success and we soon had a splendid fire going in our stove. To our eternal shame and embarrassment there was a delivery of coal to the Nissen huts the very next day. It was just as well that none of us were caught on the previous evening's escapade.

Summer 1943

The summer of 1943 produced some long spells of lovely weather. It was my first summer on the squadron and it opened up new aspects of life as an 'erk' in the RAF, especially after the tough winter that had ended earlier. I slowly became aware, however, of a sinister background that a number of my longer-serving colleagues had already experienced the previous summer. I began to realize, as they had done twelve months earlier, that these warm, balmy evenings constituted a sort or mocking backcloth for a number of our aircrews. These idyllic conditions could forecast for them a night of fear, suffering and possible death. One particular summer evening could be the last that some of them would experience on this planet or at least in this country for several years. Mercifully, our losses were still relatively small. We desperately wished to be able to contrive some sort of protective screen for our aircrews on their ops. This was impossible, of course, and all we could offer were our acquired skills and our dedication.

One of the occupants of the Nissen hut next to ours had been lucky enough to bring back from home a fairly small 'all mains' wireless receiver. These receivers were designed to operate on either AC (alternating current) mains or DC (direct current) mains. This meant that they contained no mains transformer and this resulted in their being smaller, lighter and somewhat less expensive than 'AC only' receivers. Before the war, and for some years after, a number of areas of this country were supplied with DC mains, but these were gradually converted to AC and by the late fifties most of this country had been standardized at 240 volts AC. During those warm summer evenings we could hear requested gramophone records being broadcast from the hut next door. A lot of them were songs from Fred Astaire musicals and Betty Grable films, but the most frequently played tune was, by far, the Inkspots singing 'Whispering Grass'. It seemed a most appropriate song during those lovely summer evenings.

Norman, our Corporal Wireless Mechanic on B flight, who was a super bloke, had been a sales rep before joining up. He had a very confidential, intimate way of conversing with people. Inevitably his nickname soon became 'Whispering Grass'.

Each autumn, however, this 'rotten swine' of a bloke used to arrange for himself a trip, complete with parachute, of course, on a test flight in an aircraft from B flight. The object of this was to enable him to map out all the local orchards so that he could engage in efficient night time 'scrumping' raids.

Good old Norman. I recall that at about this time I was keen on teaching myself Spanish. I happened to mention this to him and after his very next leave he brought back and sold me his copy of a Spanish-English dictionary at a price favourable to himself. I still have this dictionary but, unfortunately, my attempt to teach myself Spanish was not very successful.

One morning I called in at the main dispersal hut on A Flight to find out if there had been any late reports of W/T faults on our aircraft. There was only the corporal-fitter from G-George there. He was about ten years older than myself and, as all was well, we had a quick chat. The conversation got round to popular tunes and songs. It quickly emerged that his favourite song was the popular 'J'attendrai' sung by Jean Sablon. This corporal was terribly frustrated, however, because although this song had struck some sympathetic chord within him he didn't really know what it was about. Grabbing a piece of chalk I wrote the words of the French song on the blackboard that was normally used for jotting down such details as petrol load for each aircraft on the Flight. I then slowly translated the song into English line by line and I shall never forget his look of wonderment and gratitude as he discovered for the first time just what his favourite song meant.

Our Canadian radar mechanics

We had three or four Canadian radar mechanics in our billet. They were wonderful company, both cheerful and generous. They provided a special interest for me as one of my mother's brothers had been settled in Vancouver since 1920. At frequent intervals they received superb food parcels from home which they enthusiastically shared with the rest of us in the billet. This was my introduction to the new commodity known as peanut butter. The importance of the larger pats of butter at teatime began to fade somewhat as we now had something else available to spread on an extra slice of bread. I remember apologizing to these Canadians for the severe austerity of the wartime conditions in this country and pointing out that things had not always been like this. One other luxury that their food parcels provided was a generous supply of superb cigarettes called 'Sweet Caporal'. These were manufactured from pure Virginia tobacco. For some considerable time the tobacco of our cigarettes had been 'spiked' with additions of Greek and Turkish tobacco because of the difficulties of wartime purchasing and transport and it was an unbelievable luxury to smoke pure Virginia tobacco again.

The WAAFS

I feel that it is about time I mentioned our WAAFS. They were a welcome addition to our squadron and worked diligently and efficiently as transport drivers, in the parachute section and admin offices, etc. Their presence certainly helped us to curb some of our more colourful language. It was rather like having one's own sister around who could keep a watchful eye on us. Swearing, of course, was one of the commodities that could not be rationed by the authorities and I am afraid that many of us were coarsened by the war conditions, and it took several years of Civvy Street after the war to settle down and become more civilized. The WAAFS, of course, 'had eyes' for our superb aircrews much more than for us ground crews, but we did not begrudge them this privilege. The girls also played a noble part in the drama group and helped to produce and took part in two excellent plays at camp under very difficult conditions.

The WAAF Welfare Officer was a superb person, probably in her early forties. Like many thousands of other women of her generation she had suffered the loss of her fiancé who was killed in the First World War and she was grateful for the chance to do her bit in the Second World War. During her earlier years she had trained at the Royal Academy of Dramatic Art. It was she who founded the drama group on the squadron. I feel almost ashamed to admit that I became, unwittingly, a member of this group. I hasten to point out that I was 'conned', right from the start, by the assistant producer. He approached me and explained that one of the male cast was in sick bay and as it was important to get rehearsals under way he asked me, with some urgency, if I would sit in temporarily and read the part of this character. Being as green as they come (I was just twenty-one then) I agreed with certain misgivings. These evening rehearsals were not easy for we were all tired after a day's slog out on the aerodrome. After a week or two I began to become suspicious about the authenticity of this character who was supposed to be in sick bay, but by then I had become completely wrapped up in this new world of drama.

Our Welfare Officer, by virtue of her experience and expertise, was superb in explaining and demonstrating the basics of movement and speech on stage. Our first play was a drawing-room comedy called *George and Margaret* and in one scene I had to play the piano and indulge in several lines of dialogue with one of the other characters. Luckily, I had been taught the piano as a child but I found it terribly difficult to play and speak my lines at the same time. It was decided that to make things easier I should play a slow sonata by Beethoven. Each evening, for a couple of weeks before the first night, I sneaked into the canteen before official opening time and ploughed my way through this sonata time after time until I could play it with my eyes shut. It must have driven the canteen girls to distraction as they busied themselves with the tea urns and the slices of cake. We put the play on for two consecutive nights and it was a huge success. I was fearful of being 'ragged' by the other lads, but not a bit of it, for everyone enjoyed it immensely as it was a new experience for the squadron. The canteen girls assured me that all was forgiven after seeing and hearing the results of my labours.

Our next play was a more ambitious affair. It was a mystery thriller by Emlyn Williams called *A Murder has been Arranged*. We waded into rehearsals with renewed confidence after our recent success. With this particular production, however, there was an unusual sort of snag. Two of the male cast were aircrew and we could never be certain, after each rehearsal, if they would still be 'with us' for the next one. I am quite sure that anyone reading this who is, or has been, a member of an amateur dramatic society, will appreciate the unusual sort of suspense that this situation presented. But, of course, this was the way that things had to proceed during the war. I am delighted to report that these two members of aircrew not only survived long enough to take part in the play but also continued to complete their stint of Pathfinder ops.

The second act of this play required historical costumes to be worn by some of the members of both male and female cast. These were duly ordered on hire from Moss Bros. in London. About four days before the first night of the play the men's costumes duly arrived, but, with only two days to go, most of the girl's costumes had not materialized. A frantic phone call to London failed to produce any positive information. The drama group felt shattered and our first reaction was that the play would have to be cancelled. Then, someone had the brilliantly simple idea of obtaining from the squadron stores sufficient black-out curtain material for the girls to cut out and sew their own costumes. The girls worked late into the night and it was a wonderful demonstration of their enthusiasm and resourcefulness. The two performances of the play were a resounding success and nobody in the audience even suspected the origin of some of the girl's costumes in the second act. This drama group activity took place during the autumn of 1943. With D-Day approaching, 1944 became so hectic, with everyone stretched to the limit of their endurance, that it was impossible for the drama group to start up again. Anyway, it was good to be able to look back on the previous autumn and remember the tremendous amount of enjoyment we were able to pass on to the squadron.

The Mark III Halifax

As we went about our daily inspections of the aircraft on our own particular flight we had to cover a lot of ground as the aircraft were dispersed in 'staggered' positions over a large area of the aerodrome. As we approached each aircraft there were usually other tradesmen carrying out their own inspection and testing, and quite frequently engines were being revved up. We had discovered early on that a chap of average height could walk quite safely beneath the rotating propellers of the Mark II Halifax and this is what a lot of us always did when making our way to a particular aircraft so as to avoid a long detour.

Round about November 1943 our squadron was equipped with the new Mark III Halifax. They were magnificent aircraft and we were all delighted with them. The next morning I approached the first aircraft on our flight, ready to carry out the usual daily inspection. All four engines were being revved up. No doubt the engine fitters were having a thorough work-out so as to accustom themselves to the new radial engines and their controls.

From sheer force of habit I walked towards the rapidly rotating propellers with the intention of passing safely underneath them. As I got near them I suddenly felt a huge gust of air around my head. I remember cringing back in horror and bewilderment. This reflex action saved my life, for if I had gone forward another foot or two I would have been killed instantly. The propellers of these new radial engines were much longer than those fitted to the Merlin engines of the Mark II Halifax. They were also paddle shaped at the tips as opposed to the more pointed shape of the Merlin propellers. I never made that mistake again, although a few months later our squadron was to undergo yet another change of aircraft.

100-octane petrol

Our bombers used 100-octane petrol and there was always a busy daily scene of petrol bowsers coming round to refuel each aircraft. We always knew there was a long distance op due to take place when the blackboard in the main dispersal hut had the maximum petrol load, 2,200 gallons, chalked up opposite each aircraft. We normally managed to scrounge a few buckets of petrol for our own use. This petrol was needed to refuel our cigarette lighters, clean our overalls, wash our bicycle chains and 'dirty' petrol was used to light the stove in our dispersal hut. As it was impossible to purchase new bicycle chains it was important to lavish much care on our existing ones. We used to wash them in petrol at frequent intervals and then heat them up carefully in a shallow metal tray containing lubricating oil.

The lighting of the stove in our dispersal hut was quite a special performance. This particular stove was square in shape with two hinged doors in front and the usual chimney pipe going up through the roof. Arriving at the hut on a freezing winter morning, often in the small hours, it was important to get some heat going as quickly as possible. We stuffed paper, wood and coal into the stove and then poured a liberal quantity of dirty petrol over these contents. We then retreated to the rear portion of the hut as our stove-lighting expert took charge. Striding to within a few feet of the stove he would pause and, striking a match, flick it with unerring accuracy straight through the open doors of the stove. There followed a muffled explosion with the stove doors flapping in and out rapidly like a demented cuckoo clock. Then, with burning petrol trickling through on to the concrete floor below, the stove sprang into life with a mighty roar and was soon giving our splendid heat. We used to huddle round the stove for a few precious minutes before setting out on our various duties around the Flight.

The 'Instrument Bashers'

This was the nickname, totally undeserved, given to the Instrument Repair Section. Most of their members consisted of older, experienced watchmakers. I spent many a happy hour, during stand-by night duty, in the inner sanctum of their workshop, observing skilled watchmakers going about their tasks. This, for me, was a privilege that is still available today for any young man or woman in the RAF. In those days this privilege could only be earned after many months of hard endeavour, demonstrating beyond doubt that one could 'muck-in' and collaborate with anyone and everyone. I used to marvel at the precision and delicacy with which they dismantled the tiny parts of a watch or clock movement. Wind-up spring watches were the only type available then and, quite naturally, there was a heavy and constant demand for repairs, both official and private, to watches and clocks. With concrete floors being the order of the day the majority of watch casualties resulted from the accidental dropping of these watches. The delicate balance staff pivots snapped off and no amount of devoted shaking would coax the watch back into a healthy, obedient ticking.

No watchmaker lathes were available on squadrons during wartime austerity but I used to observe, spellbound, as balance staff pivots were turned by hand until they became almost invisible to the naked eye. I acquired and assimilated a tremendous amount of technique that stood me in good stead throughout my working life as a technician.

We change over to Lancasters

One afternoon in March 1944 we were working as usual on our Mark III Halifaxes when the sky above the aerodrome suddenly became black with circling aircraft. Even more intriguing, they began to land in quick succession and we could then see that they were brand new Lancasters. We were quickly summoned over to our main dispersal huts and informed over the tannoy that the squadron was about to change over to Lancasters and we had precisely twenty-four hours in which to get them completely operational including the fitting of all the modifications necessary for Pathfinder work. It was fortunate that most of us were young for we had a long slog ahead of us. The comradeship that we ground crews had developed certainly bore fruit, for there were occasions when several of us were literally standing on each other's bodies in order to reach the same area of a particular aircraft to carry out the necessary modifications according to our trade. I need hardly add that a portion of the twenty-four hours allotted to us had to be used for brief test flights by our aircrews to accustom themselves to the new Lancasters. The following evening, tired, dishevelled but triumphant, we stood and watched as our squadron of brand new Lancasters took off on their first Pathfinder op.

To be honest, it took us quite a long time to 'accept' the Lancasters. They were excellent aircraft, of course, but we had become so besotted with our Halifaxes, especially since our acquisition of the Mark III just four months earlier, that we felt our loyalty had been put under unfair stress. The grapevine, of course, quickly pointed out that the other Pathfinder squadrons, who had always been equipped with Lancasters, had put in a concerted complaint to No. 8 headquarters during the previous November after we had received our Mark III Halifaxes. Apparently, according to the grapevine, the Lancasters of the other Pathfinder squadrons had experienced considerable difficulty in matching the speed of our new Halifaxes and, as it was vital for our squadrons to rendezvous over the target area within seconds, then something drastic had to be done. Be that as it may, one thing was for sure — D-Day couldn't be very far away.

The Electricians

I discovered, during my service in the RAF and subsequent decades in Civvy Street, that electricians are excellent fellows, but, for one reason or another, have always appeared to experience more than their fair share of worries. I have already described the bombing-up procedure, pointing out that bomb doors were always left open until the last moment before each aircraft started to taxi round the perimeter track ready for take-off. The electricians could often be heard, during the course of daily inspections, bewailing the fact that they had discovered a 'rogue earth return' to one of the bomb carrier solenoids on a particular aircraft. I will explain the significance of this as briefly as possible: One terminal of each aircraft accumulator was connected in turn to one end of each bomb release solenoid. The other terminal of the accumulator was connected, as in the motor car, to 'earth', or, in other words, to the metal bodywork of the aircraft. When the bomb aimer pressed the button of his bomb release switch, this switch would, according to which bomb carrier he had selected by means of a multi-way switch, connect (or complete) the necessary earth return to that particular solenoid. The solenoid would then be energized by the accumulator and the solenoid hook withdrawn, magnetically, from the ring on the bomb which fell immediately under the force of gravity. If there had been a 'rogue earth return' to one of the bomb carrier solenoids, independent of the bomb aimer's release switch, then the bomb attached to that particular carrier would drop the moment the aircraft battery was switched on. Bearing in mind that the bomb doors were always left open until the last moment, it becomes apparent that any last-minute adjustment to W/T equipment requiring the switching-on of the accumulator was a tense and worrying experience. It became more so during the second half of 1944 when our squadron started to use lots of delayed-action bombs to attack U-boat pens and also introduced the Master Bomber technique. I am delighted to report that our splendid electricians always managed to correct all 'rogue earths' and we never had any accidents involving the random release of a bomb.

The delayed action bomb quickly acquired considerable notoriety. It was difficult for bomb armourers to handle and the fuse mechanism was ultra-sensitive to vibration. The grapevine conveyed several reports of ghastly accidents that other squadrons had experienced with them. If I remember correctly, these bombs had two coloured bands, one red and the other green, painted on them close to the tail fin. Whenever we had last-minute adjustments to make to our equipment we shone our torch through the slots in the floor immediately above the bomb bay and if we saw the red and green bands of delayed action bombs leering back at us our hearts missed several beats as we switched on the accumulator.

By a strange quirk of fate I worked alongside one of the technologists involved in the development of the delayed action bomb. This was some ten years or so after the war. He had been drafted into Farnborough, along with other technologists, to work on a crash programme of research and development of the delayed action bomb. As he explained, they were given very little time to come up with an answer as the need to bomb the U-boat pens had become terribly urgent.

I mentioned, just now, the switching on of the aircraft accumulator. This action, in fact, was a privilege accorded only to those of us who consistently collaborated with and helped the electricians whenever possible. They were responsible for the condition of each aircraft's accumulator and their permission to use the accumulator had to be constantly sought after. The stark alternative was to use the 'chore-horse'. This consisted of a two-wheel trolley on which was fitted a small petrol engine driving a dynamo to charge a large accumulator. The engine had to be started by wrapping several turns of cord around the flywheel and tugging smartly on the cord, just like today's outboard motors. Then there was the enormously thick output cable, terminating in a huge bronze-encased two pin plug, that had to be manhandled. Before all this, of course, the 'chore-horse' had to be hauled across mud that could be either squelching or frozen hard so that the bronze plug could be pushed into the socket, fitted with a spring loaded cover, that was built into the fuselage close to the nose of the aircraft. When I tell you that this activity frequently took place late at night with a thick hoar-frost covering everything, I am sure you will appreciate that it was a wonderful privilege and luxury to be given permission by the electrician to use the aircraft accumulator for a few minutes of tuning up transmitters and receivers.

A sad occasion for our Corporal

It was May 1944 and the *Luftwaffe* had finally been shot out of the sky over France. Bomber Command began to mix daylight raids with the usual night bombing. Our Corporal on A Flight was a splendid chap called John. He was a schoolmaster, about ten years or so older than myself and a quiet, efficient wireless mechanic. He suddenly received a telegram from his home town in the Potteries informing him that his wife, who was in the late stages of pregnancy, was desperately ill and the doctors had serious doubts about her chances of survival. John was immediately granted a few days of compassionate leave. The following morning I rose early at about 6.30 a.m. busying myself as quietly as possible so as not to disturb our sleeping colleagues, to prepare coffee with a simple breakfast for John, using some of the 'goodies' I had managed to scrounge from the cookhouse the previous evening. John, meanwhile, was quietly making preparations to set off on his bicycle to catch the early morning train heading north from the village station of Offord. Although it was May the weather was dull, chilly and uninviting. I remember thinking how often our weather seemed to reflect our sombre personal experiences. John had his breakfast and coffee and, with his face looking grey and drawn with anxiety, set off on his bicycle.

My other wireless mechanic colleague on A Flight was a grand chap called Harold. He was about the same age as John and, like him, was a schoolmaster. He was short, plump and round-faced and came from Hereford. He had made a lifetime study of the Music Hall and gave many excellent, impromptu impersonations of leading artists. Unfortunately, at this particular time, he was confined to sick quarters with tonsillitis. This meant that I was now the only available wireless mechanic on A Flight. The significance of this quickly became apparent as Bomber Command began to combine daylight raids on French territory with their usual night raids on German targets. For several nights I slept rough on a bench in the dispersal hut, so that I would be available immediately to 'see in' the aircraft of A Flight from their early morning raid and get first-hand information about any faults or flak damage that had occurred during the op. This was vitally important as the aircraft had to be made serviceable for evening take-off. Eight Lancasters presented a daunting task for one lone wireless mechanic. Luckily, Harold finally emerged from sick bay and the following day John returned, still looking worried but less strained. The baby had been lost, but mercifully his wife's life had been saved. I have often thought about John and his wife over the years and found myself hoping that they finally managed to start a family safely, for he was such a superb individual.

The return of John and Harold was timely indeed, for within a day or two we were into D-Day. On the morning of 6th June we saw in our aircraft from their now customary early morning raid on French territory. As the aircrews scrambled out of their bombers they called out to us 'the invasion is under way!' Less than an hour earlier, on their return flight, they had flown over the huge allied armada on its way to Normandy. We were probably among the first of 'normal mortals' to hear this exciting news. We suddenly realized that the past months of non-stop slog were now beginning to pay off in earnest. Morale shot sky-high and we redoubled our efforts under this wonderful new stimulus. Within a few weeks of this new situation Bomber Command stepped up its bombing campaign with increased intensity against German industrial targets. No. 8 Pathfinder Group introduced its new bombing technique — the Master Bombers.

Master Bombers

The basic plan was that each Pathfinder squadron appointed a Master Bomber along with deputy Master Bombers in case of accidents, whose duty was to stooge around the target area directing operations by wireless communication. The technological aspect of this new system was simplicity itself. The bombers simply used their existing short range transmitter/receivers that were normally brought into operation on returning to base to contact the control tower for instructions regarding landing procedure. These transmitter/receivers operated on four crystal-controlled frequencies, channels A, B, C and D, selected by push-button switches. Channel A was normally tuned to the frequency (or wavelength) of the transmitter/receiver installed in the squadron's control tower. Channel D was tuned, in all aircraft of Bomber Command, to the universal 'distress' frequency so that any bomber returning from an op in some sort of trouble could call up the control tower of the nearest aerodrome and ask for landing instructions. This left channels B and C available for any other frequency setting that might be required.

Before anyone who happens to read this begins to feel that he or she is being dragged down into the murky depths of technology, I would simply point out that every battery-operated watch and clock in use today is fitted with precisely the same type of quartz crystal (although much smaller) as we used during the war. These were enclosed in moulded Bakelite housings measuring about two inches by one inch.

They had two plug-in pins attached to the base, which were connected internally to the two opposite faces of the thin-rectangular 'slice' of quartz crystal. The exciting property of these crystals is that once a small voltage is applied between the opposite faces the crystal oscillates at a stable frequency that is dependent almost solely on its physical size, hence the accurate time-keeping of the modern battery-operated watch and clock.

As far as we wireless mechanics were concerned, the introduction of the Master Bomber technique meant that about an hour before take-off a despatch rider roared up to the guardroom on his motor bike and handed in a linen bag containing the plug-in crystals for that night's op. These crystals were handed over to the W/T section and we set off on our rounds plugging in these crystals and tuning the TR1196 on each aircraft to this new frequency. On each Master Bomber raid a new frequency of transmission and reception was selected.

In future, as you consult your quartz-controlled watch, admiring its superb time-keeping if not its general appearance, perhaps you will feel a glow of pride and gratitude in the knowledge that your watch is using part of the same basic technology employed in the transmitter/receivers that enabled our incredibly brave aircrews to communicate with each other over the target area.

Earlier on, in mentioning the technique of the Master Bombers, I went into considerable detail about the transmitter/receivers our bombers pressed into service for this long series of operations. Each one of our fighter aircraft was equipped with a similar, crystal-controlled transmitter/receiver. It was, however, a more powerful set with a much longer range of communication, and so my remarks about feelings of pride and gratitude in conjunction with crystal-controlled watches, apply equally to our superb fighter pilots!

Quite frequently there was the now familiar last minute change of bomb load. The swearing armourer could often be heard on these occasions at a nearby aircraft. It was strangely comforting and reassuring to hear him 'letting rip', for, in the cold and dark recesses of a huge bomber there was a feeling of remoteness, working with the aid of a slowly fading beam of light from a hand torch, especially knowing that just a few inches beneath one's feet the bomb bay was crammed with a formidable load of assorted bombs. The bomb bay doors were still open and the aircraft accumulators switched on while we worked urgently to re-tune the TR1196. God bless all RAF electricians for eradicating unwanted 'earth returns' from bomb carrier release solenoids. Sadly, the losses on Pathfinder squadrons increased considerably with the introduction of the Master Bomber technique and the summer months of 1944 were much grimmer than those of 1943. The *Luftwaffe* had withdrawn its remaining fighter squadrons to Germany and equipped them with sophisticated radar equipment turning them into formidable night fighters.

Driving at last

At some stage during 1944 I learned to drive our W/T van. Sheer desperation had impelled me to this drastic action. It became apparent over several months that I had become doomed to finding myself stuck at the dispersal hut of A Flight usually about teatime, with a transmitter or some other piece of heavy equipment that needed overhauling. I used to contact the W/T section on the field telephone and then wait with increasing impatience for some kindly soul to drive round, realizing that with every passing minute the larger pats of butter were being snapped up!

When delivering heavy transmitters, etc. to aircraft we always reversed the van to within a few feet of the entrance hatch to ensure that we didn't have to carry the heavy equipment an inch further than necessary. In the case of our Halifaxes, this entailed reversing the tall van carefully underneath the wing just beyond the port outer engine. It was a tricky operation because the two offside wheels of the van were on the concrete of the dispersal pan whilst the two nearside wheels were on the mud beyond the dispersal pan and that mud could be either wet and squelchy or frozen hard and rutted. When we received our new Lancasters in March 1944, we discovered that the entrance hatch was on the starboard side of the fuselage as opposed to the port side of the Halifaxes: it took us some weeks to get used to this and many a time we would carefully reverse the van round to the port side of an aircraft only to realize at the last moment that we had arrived at the 'blank' side of the aircraft.

Food parcels for Holland

Round about April 1945 news reached this country that people in some areas of Holland were literally starving as a result of the recent Nazi occupation and the various ravages they had inflicted on that country. It was decided at once to drop food parcels to the affected areas and Pathfinder squadrons were selected initially to carry out this operation as a result of their superb record of high precision navigation. It was a novel but uplifting experience to help load these food parcels into our bombers. As a point of interest my wife has a Dutch woman friend who has lived in this country for a number of years now and was a schoolgirl in Holland at that time. She vividly remembers the excitement of seeing hundreds of food parcels parachuting down around her home. Well done, the RAF, yet again!

VE Day

Many of the older people in this country will remember VE day as a time of excited rejoicing and street parties. For those of us in the Armed Services, stationed in the remoter areas of the country, it was just another day. There was a feeling of immense relief, of course; the summer weather was lovely and I remember writing to my parents congratulating them on having survived the blitz and the war in general. There still remained the threat of Japan and a lot of my colleagues suddenly found themselves transferred into the Royal Navy and the Fleet Air Arm, ready for the final assault on Japan. Most of them were still on embarkation leave when the first atom bomb fell on Hiroshima, quickly followed by the second on Nagasaki. The war was over but for us it was a rather muddled and confused ending. Our squadron had been split up but at least we could look forward to peace in our time.

After VJ day a lot of our 'veteran' aircrews were released from the RAF. A large proportion of pilots and flight engineers went into Civil Aviation, where, of course, they were welcomed with open arms. New young aircrews and ground crews were posted to the squadron because, of course, the relentless process of preparation and training had to continue. The Berlin airlift of 1949, for example, was the first proof of the wisdom of this strategy. Practice bombing at a nearby bombing range became the new daily routine. The rigorous daily inspections of all aircraft continued and no aircraft was allowed to take off unless and until the daily inspection certificate for that particular aircraft had been duly signed by all the tradesmen concerned. The practice bombs were small, slim and painted white. They looked puny in comparison with the huge wartime bombs we had become accustomed to. There was one noticeable difference surrounding this new form of daily activity. There were no more last-minute changes in bomb load and so there were no more opportunities for our swearing armourer to 'let rip'. It so happened that he was released from the RAF just a few weeks after VJ day. He was sorely missed on A flight.

I have been using the term 'release' and perhaps I should explain in more detail. After VJ day there was no demobilization of our armed forces, only release. There was Class A release, based on age plus length of service and Class B release that applied mainly to older men such as schoolteachers, fitters, turners and instrument makers, etc., who were already fully trained and skilled in their trade or profession. These men were released quickly so as to get this country back on its feet as soon as possible. These two categories of release were fair and universally popular. I never heard a single word of dissent. As the State of Emergency that was declared in 1938/39 was not, and never has been, declared 'over' by an Order in Council, it meant that officially we were still members of the particular branch of the armed forces we had joined during the war and could be recalled for service if the need arose. I still possess my Release Book that contains, among other items, a one-way travel warrant that can be presented to British Rail in the unlikely event of my recall. Over the years I have cherished the knowledge that I could still be needed. I still consider that I am a member of the RAF. My generation, however, has always hoped and prayed that there would be no more wars.

A number of other developments occurred on our squadron. Firstly, the NAAFI inaugurated a mobile canteen van that drove round every morning to each of the three flights in turn. Next, we took delivery of a brand new W/T van. It seemed ironic that we had to struggle during wartime with a 'clapped-out' van that was a real beast to get started, especially on a cold winter morning. Although there had always been a speed limit of 15 m.p.h. imposed on vehicles using the perimeter track, our new W/T van was always the first to reach the mobile canteen each morning. The methods we used to achieve this record must remain a

State secret, I'm afraid, but it gave us the opportunity to fill our huge thermos flask with freshly brewed tea and also the first pickings of the slices of Madeira cake — the 'yellow peril' as we used to call it, somewhat unfairly.

Another development was the issue of newly designed battledress uniform to ground crews. This was much more practical than the traditional type that had been issued previously. Firstly, there were no more brass buttons that had to be polished each day. Secondly, the jacket had two capacious breast pockets that were invaluable to tradesmen for stowing away small hand tools. Our aircrews were green with envy and protested until they were rewarded with their own issue and rightly so. We were quite sure, initially, that this was due to occur in any case, but it was a perfect demonstration of the instant popularity of this new battledress. At the time is seemed a great pity that these innovations had to wait until after the wartime slog had ended, but then wartime had been dogged by inescapable austerity and restrictions.

Finally, our squadron — No. 35 — was selected to go on a goodwill tour of the USA. The Lancasters were painted white in readiness. There was one big snag. Those who volunteered to go would have to postpone their release from the RAF for an indefinite period. For me, and lots of others, this was a bit too much and we decided not to go. For a time I regretted this decision but, on reflection later on, I realized that had I gone, the course of my life would have changed completely and I would never have met my wife.

A word of advice

I would like to say to any young man or woman who happens to be reading this booklet and who hasn't been able, as yet, to decide in which direction their career should start, to think long and hard about applying to one of our Armed Services. They all offer a wide range of interesting careers. If you apply and are accepted you receive an immediate double bonus. Firstly, you will know that you are medically fit and, secondly, you will receive the finest training that is available in this country. You will be well paid and will enjoy wonderful comradeship together with shared joys, sorrows and any dangers that happen to loom up in the future. I can virtually guarantee that the pats of butter will not only be of identical size but also will almost certainly be wrapped in foil. I am also quite sure that you will not need to raid the camp's coal dump (if, indeed, it has one!) in order to provide a bit of heating for your living quarters. So, if you reckon that you have 'got what it takes' and especially if you have performed well at school, then, go on, have a bash! My generation, or at least what is left of us, would like to feel, as the shadows lengthen around us, that our Armed Forces will be strong and well trained, ready to meet any emergency that may occur in the future. One final word of advice — make sure you know the colour of your eyes!

Fighter Command

In Bomber Command we were always acutely aware of the fact that if it hadn't been for the fantastic bravery, heroism and sacrifices of the wonderful young men and women of Fighter Command then this country would have been overrun by Nazi Germany and there would have been no role left either for Bomber Command or any of our other Armed Services. I would imagine that the time factor imposed on ground crews of Fighter Command was much more hectic than we experienced on bomber squadrons. I sincerely hope that there are still lots of our Battle of Britain colleagues still going strong and I also hope that if any of them have managed to wade through this rambling booklet I will have rung a few bells of memory for them. Looking back at the RAF over the years one finds a wonderfully consistent thread of quiet efficiency bonding it together.

Long live the Royal Air Force.

A sad pilgrimage

One blazing hot Saturday in June 1948 I set off early from Elstree and cycled the fifty or so miles to Graveley to take another look at the old place. Arriving hot and tired I sank down gratefully into the long grass near the edge of the deserted aerodrome. After a while my thoughts and memories started to drift back over a few years to those hectic days on this very site and I found myself listening intently for the sound of the Merlin engines of our aircraft and the shouts, laughs and curses. Above all I listened for the precious sound of our aircraft returning from an op, hoping to be able to count them back in carefully. It was all in vain, for the only sound was that of the summer breeze ruffling the long grass. It was good to know that the war was now well and truly over, but, sad to report, none of our missing aircraft and crews returned to Graveley on that particular afternoon.

The photograph on the front (sorry about that!) was taken round about August 1942. I was at home on a few days' leave after completing a six months' stint as an acting, paid Corporal Instructor on the first part of the Wireless/Radar Mechanics course. The stripes had to be removed, of course, before I set off to complete the second part of the course.

RAF No. 1434622

El color de la música

El color de la música

Javier Gregori

Dairea

Colección Mvsica Libraria ML01

El color de la música
© Del texto, Javier Gregori
© De las ilustraciones, Juan Antonio Peña y Sara Peña Martín
© De la presente edición, DAIREA Ediciones
Consilia Musicorum S.L.
Silva, 2 – 3º, 1. 28013 Madrid
+34 91 222 2112
www.daireaediciones.es

Diseño de cubierta y maquetación: Daniel de Labra

Impreso en COIMPRESS.
San Romualdo, 26. 28037 Madrid
+34 91 327 2160

ISBN: 978-84-939672-0-8
Depósito legal: M-45829-2011

A la memoria de Rosa María Belda,
la voz más cálida y hermosa de la radio

Mi padre cumplió su amenaza. Un buen día me dijo:
–Oye, Pilar, ¿no te gustaría ir al campo de vacaciones?
¿Al campo?

Horror. Moscas, mosquitos y avispas. Escorpiones y serpientes. Hormigas rojas, babosas, abejorros, cucarachas...Y lo peor de todo: las arañas. Las hay de todos los tipos y colores: con la cabezota grande y las piernas delgadas, con la cabeza fina y los brazos gordos llenos de pelos. Grises, negras, pardas, amarillas... ¿Amarillas? ¿Arañas amarillas... o son los sapos los que son amarillos? ¡Qué más da! A los bichitos no les basta con subir y pisotearte toda la espalda. Claro, además tienen que picarte y, luego, te sale un grano rojo, aquello empieza a hincharse y desde ese momento solo tienes un pensamiento en la cabeza:

¡¡¡RASCARTE!!!

Resumiendo: ¿a alguien se le ocurre un lugar más asqueroso que el campo para ir de vacaciones?

–Si apruebas todas las asignaturas –mi padre volvía a la carga–, te prometo que este verano pasaremos unos días en la casa rural de tu tío.

Más que una promesa aquello era toda una amenaza.

A partir de ese momento, todos mis esfuerzos se concentraron en un único y gran objetivo: suspender el curso. Cambié el orden de los resultados de los problemas en el examen de matemáticas, copié un cuadro de Picasso en el trabajo de fin de curso de Plástica y, por si no fuera bastante, en la última prueba de Lengua, contesté la pregunta siete como si fuera la tres y la nueve por la siete.

–¿Tres sobresalientes? –mi padre no podía creérselo cuando abrió el boletín de notas y... yo tampoco. ¡Algo había fallado en mi plan!–. Se nota que tienes ganas de ir de vacaciones al campo –concluyó.

Otra vez el campo. Mi padre se estaba poniendo muy pesado con eso de pasar unos días en el campo. Yo traté de quitarle la idea como pude:

–Papi, me duele mucho la barriga.

Ni caso. Bueno, he de reconocer que esto estaba un poco visto.

–Papá –me esmeré dos horas después–, recuerda que soy alérgica al polen del abeto.

Segundo error: papá es aficionado a la jardinería (nosotros, que ni siquiera tenemos terraza en el minipiso en el que vivimos) y me explica pacientemente que la polinización solo se produce en primavera. Eso pasa por poner la clase de ciencias a primera hora de la mañana del lunes, casi siempre me quedo dormida y llego tarde.

–Padre mío –intenté desesperadamente por la noche–, he de comunicarte que el profe de Ciencias Naturales nos ha prohibido pisar el césped para no machacar a los múltiples animalillos que viven en él.

Ninguna reacción. Encefalograma plano. Papá siempre acaba roncando en el sofá cuando ponen en la tele una peli de policías.

A la mañana siguiente, mi padre metió cuatro cosas en una maleta y allá que nos fuimos.

–Seguro que te gustará la nueva casa que el hermano mayor de tu madre se ha construido él solo en mitad del bosque –me decía mientras arrancaba el coche, se saltaba un par de semáforos en rojo y casi se llevaba por delante a una abuelita muy simpática que intentaba cruzar la calle por un paso de cebra.

–Mamá y yo tenemos que trabajar todo el mes, pero en el campo estarás bien –continuó diciendo mi padre sin percatarse de que la viejecita en cuestión le estaba mandando a freír espárragos–. Allí el aire está limpio y se come muy bien: judías verdes, coles, zanahorias, guisantes...

¿Guisantes? Puaff. Ni caso. Yo, por mi parte, abrí la ventanilla del asiento de atrás, sin que se diera cuenta, y comencé a poner cara de susto a todos los automovilistas que se cruzaban en nuestro camino. Tenía la esperanza de que alguno creyera que estaba siendo raptada por un maníaco sexual y que llamara a la policía para que detuviera el coche de mi padre. Pero lo único que conseguí es que un guardia con bigotes nos pusiera una multa porque no me había colocado el cinturón de seguridad. ¡Cómo iba a ponérmelo si estaba fingiendo un secuestro! Los policías de tráfico es que no tienen imaginación.

Cuando el agente se fue, mi padre me echó el papel de la multa a la cara y soltó varios tacos mientras quitaba el freno de mano del coche para reiniciar el viaje. Pero no me desanimé. Utilicé entonces toda mi fuerza mental, que es mucha, para ordenarle a una piedra puntiaguda que pinchara una rueda. O mejor, dos. A ser posible, las delanteras, y lo hubiera logrado si, en ese mismo instante, una moto no hubiera dado un patinazo y se hubiera incrustado en nuestro maletero, con el piloto y todo. Os juro que yo no tuve nada que ver con este último incidente, pero mi padre me sacó del coche a empujones y me sentó en la cuneta encima de un bote oxidado de tomate frito que alguien había arrojado el verano pasado.

–Tengo que esperar a la ambulancia para que recoja lo poco que ha quedado de este motero miope –me advirtió mi progenitor–. Además, no creo que esta antigualla de coche pueda volver a arrancar nunca más después del trancazo que le han dado –sentenció.

¡Fantástico! Por fin mi plan anticampo había funcionado. Aprovechando el desconcierto del accidente, pensaba introducirme debajo de la camilla y, cuando mi padre se diera cuenta, ya estaría de vuelta en la ciudad jugando a las cartas con el enfermero y ganando toda una fortuna. Después me iría a un Casino, me jugaría todas mis ganancias en la ruleta rusa y me convertiría en la mujer más rica del mundo. Compraría un yate transoceánico, recorrería todas las playas del Caribe y le enviaría una foto a mis padres bañándome entre tiburones y arrecifes de coral. Y detrás escribiría con letras mayúsculas: "Estas sí que son unas vacaciones, so burros".

El final, sin embargo, fue bastante distinto al que yo me había imaginado. Con tres horas de retraso, llegué a la casa de campo de mi tío, más muerta que viva del cansancio y... en taxi.

Primer día en el campo. Nada de especial. No salí de la cama. Un mosquito asesino no paraba de sobrevolar mi cabeza. Si me hubiera atrevido a abandonar la protección de las sábanas, seguro que me habría acribillado a picotazos.

Segundo día. Sin novedad. Bueno sí, ahora el mosquito asesino tiene un aliado: una araña negra y grande que me mira desde el techo como si fuera su cena especial de Navidad.

Tercer día. Mi cuarto empieza a oler a muerto. Mis tíos, al ver que no salía ni a desayunar, han ido dejando encima de mi mesilla una rara colección de platos y cuencos de comida. Es toda de color verde. Por supuesto, ni la pruebo. Un día oí en la tele que a una niña la obligaron a tragarse un plato de lentejas, que le había preparado su abuela, y estuvo tres meses en coma.

Cuarto día. Magníficas noticias. El mosquito asesino ha desaparecido, pero, a cambio, una multitud de moscas ha invadido mi habitación. ¿Será porque la comida se encuentra en estado de putrefacción y hago pis en las botellas de leche que me deja mi tía?

Quinto día. Las moscas siguen ahí... y la araña también. Decido ponerme a dieta. Seguiré sin comer nada que sea de color verde, pero haré una excepción con las tostadas con mermelada de kiwi, que mi tía me pone en una bandeja para poder desayunar en la cama. Mi plan de no salir de mi habitación para no pisar el campo funciona a las mil maravillas, excepto por un pequeño detalle: mis tripas no me dejan dormir porque hacen más ruido que el camión de la basura.

Sexto día. Mi tío me ha entregado una carta de mis papás. La abro y la leo (por supuesto, en la cama):

"Querida Pilar: (ésa soy yo)

Si continúas con ese juego absurdo de no querer salir de tu cuarto, te enviaremos a tu primo Carlos para que te haga compañía".

¿Mi primo Carlos? ¿El mismo que viene todas las nochebuenas y me quema las trenzas con sus petardos y me pone trampas para cazar osos dentro de mis zapatos nuevos de fiesta? Creo que ha llegado el momento de conocer el campo.

El campo es bonito. Si no me creéis, solo hay que abrir una enciclopedia y ver una foto para poder comprobarlo, aunque no os lo recomiendo: los libros están llenos de ácaros y otros microorganismos peligrosos. Sí, es verdad, lo reconozco: el campo es bonito, pero... está completamente vacío. No hay calles, ni farolas, ni tampoco coches ni tiendas. A mi madre le encanta ir de tiendas y por eso nunca se le ocurriría ir al campo.

–¿Por qué no sales un poco a airearte? –me soltó mi tío una mañana en plena cara.

–¿Y las serpientes venenosas, qué? –le contesté yo, y me entraron una ganas enormes de retorcerle el pescuezo.

–Aquí no hay de ésas –me dijo como si tal cosa.

–¿Y plantas carnívoras?

–Tampoco, eso es en Africa, creo– y se fue a cortar unos troncos para la chimenea con un hacha tan grande y afilada que seguro que la había robado del Museo de la Tortura, donde guardan los objetos que han usado los criminales más sanguinarios de la historia.

–Tu tío tiene razón –me gritó su mujer desde el jardín. Estaba tratando de recomponer un tiesto de flores que sus gatos solían utilizar como campo de batalla–. Un poco de sol te irá bien. Últimamente te veo muy blanca.

¿Blanca? ¿No es así el color de la piel que se les pone a los muertos cuando los llevan al cementerio? Después de tres días en el campo, me sentía fatal. Sin la energía que te dan dos buenas bolsas de chucherías al día, estaba completamente perdida.

Solo me quedaba una salida: escribiría a mi abuela y le contaría que me habían encerrado en una vieja casa de madera a punto de desplomarse. Que no me daban nada de comida y que las ratas ya trepaban, con sus dientes afilados, por las patas de mi cama para poder comer algo caliente.Y era imposible escapar de allí, porque unos cocodrilos gigantescos rodeaban aquel caserón perdido en medio de un pantano de aguas pestilentes.

¡Menuda imaginación tengo yo cuando me interesa exagerar una historia!

–Los cocodrilos también están en Africa –me comentó mi tía mientras me acercaba una taza de chocolate.

¿¡Cómo diablos había podido adivinar lo de los cocodrilos¡?...

¡Menuda espía estaba hecha mi tía! Seguro que había visto el dibujo que le estaba pintando a mi abuela, para que se hiciera una pequeña idea de los peligros a los que se estaba enfrentando su querida nieta.

Mi abuela era mi última oportunidad y, al cabo de tres días de larga espera, recibí un telegrama:

"Tu abuela se ha ido de vacaciones a las Bahamas. Stop. Le daré tu carta cuando regrese dentro de tres meses. Stop. Si es que vuelve. Stop. Firmado: la vecina que le riega los cactus".

Ahora sí que estaba perdida... del todo.

–¿Por qué no te acercas al pueblo que está al otro lado del río? –volvió a la carga mi tía, una mañana interminable de aquellas– ¿O prefieres ayudarme a fregar los platos?

No lo dudé ni un segundo, mi espíritu de aventurera se impuso y abrí la puerta dispuesta a comerme el mundo.

–Con el pijama y los pies descalzos no irás muy lejos.

Ya estaba otra vez mi tío amargándome la existencia. Cuánto odiaba estar en el campo, nadie te dejaba nunca en paz.Y si no que se lo pregunten a las moscas.

Vivir en una gran ciudad tiene muchas ventajas. Bueno... algunas. Está bien, unas pocas. Vale, ¿lo dejamos, por lo menos, en una o dos?

Os lo voy a demostrar. Primera ventaja: si eres un virus malo, como el de la gripe, tienes a tu entera disposición a millones de cuerpos humanos que viven amontonados en unos pocos metros cuadrados. Por eso, durante la mayor parte del año, en la ciudad no se oyen los trinos de los pájaros, sino las toses y los estornudos de las personas que viajan en el metro o el autobús.

Segunda ventaja: la gran ciudad también es todo un paraíso para los astronautas. Los edificios son tan altos que, si quieres viajar a la Luna, te subes a uno de ellos y ya tienes buena parte del camino hecho. Y todavía me salen muchas más, por ejemplo, ducharte puede salirte gratis. Al menos, eso dice siempre mi vecino del último piso, el 14 A, que siempre se está quejando de las goteras que hay en el techo de su casa. Y digo yo, con tanta agua gratis, ¿por qué no planta césped en el salón de su casa y se dedica a jugar al golf? Seguro que así se le pasaría el mal humor.

Porque en las ciudades cualquiera puede ser feliz. Hay árboles en las aceras (si no los han arrancado antes para hacer aparcamientos para los coches), columpios en los parques (si no los han quemado los gamberros del botellón) y cines, muchos cines, con películas de tiros y puñetazos, de esas que nos gustan tanto a los niños. Yo me divierto mucho contando los muertos que salen hasta que se acaba la cinta. Mi récord está en cinco fiambres por segundo.

Por si fuera poco, en una ciudad grande nunca te aburres. Las sirenas de las ambulancias no paran de sonar y los bomberos suben y bajan por tu calle, de día y de noche, y es muy divertido ver cómo desenrollan sus mangueras y suben corriendo a los pisos mientras la gente grita desde un balcón lleno de humo. Mi padre dice que a los arquitectos de las ciudades siempre se les olvida poner escaleras de emergencia y yo me digo que será porque el hierro cuesta mucho dinero y los alcaldes de las ciudades prefieren gastar en cosas más importantes, como los campos de fútbol.

Por último, vivir en una ciudad es muy educativo. Yo no entendí qué era un número primo hasta que un hombre me pidió en la calle dinero para un bocadillo y luego le vi comprando una botella de vino en el supermercado. ¡Las cosas que se aprenden en una gran ciudad! Yo no sabría estar en otro sitio. Mis pulmones se volverían locos si, de repente, respiraran una bocanada de aire limpio. Mi corazón solo sabe latir a cien por hora, porque en las ciudades siempre hacemos las cosas deprisa y corriendo.

–¿Dónde vas, pequeña?

El panadero me sacó de mis pensamientos. En el campo no hay manera de que te dejen tranquila. Con eso de que no eres de allí, porque la cara no les suena, todos se creen que tienen derecho a pararte para preguntarte cosas realmente estúpidas.

–¿De dónde eres?

Si ya lo decía yo...

–¿Cuántos años tienes, niña?

... preguntas realmente estúpidas.

–¿Ha terminado ya el colegio?

Este panadero es un auténtico tostón. No le basta con repartir el pan cada mañana con una furgoneta medio destartalada, además tiene que incordiar a todo el mundo.

–Seguro que vienes de una ciudad grande. Lo digo por esa cara tan blanca que tienes de no tomar nunca el sol. El campo te vendrá bien, chica, aquí el aire es tan puro y el agua tan fresca que pone contentos incluso a los cuervos. Pero ¿dónde vas, chiquilla, tan sola por estos caminos?

–Para allá –le señalé el primer punto que se me ocurrió en el horizonte para que me dejara en paz.

–Allí no vive nadie. El pueblo está abandonado desde hace años.

–¿Qué pueblo? –repliqué yo. Lo único que veía a lo lejos era un par de casas de piedra con las paredes caídas y los tejados llenos de agujeros.

–No te hagas la tonta. A todos los niños de ciudad os gusta destrozar pueblos abandonados, ¿a que sí? Si lo sabré yo: arrancáis las puertas a patadas, rompéis los pocos cristales que quedan y, si os aburrís, tiráis piedras a la pobre campana de la iglesia para ver si se cae, ¿a que sí?

Vaya, el panadero es en el fondo un maldito policía.

–¿A que sí, niña de ciudad?

Niña de ciudad... y a mucha honra, que el campo está más sucio que el patio de mi colegio: hay polvo por todas partes, cagarrutas de oveja, barro, ramas caídas, hojas disecadas... ¿es que nadie piensa limpiar un poco todo esto?

–Ya lo tengo, chiquilla: te he pillado "in fraganti". Estabas planeando una gamberrada, ¿a que sí?, y por eso te has quedado más muda que una mula sorda.

¿En qué quedamos?, ¿la mula está sorda... o muda? Este panadero–policía no tiene arreglo: ve delincuentes por todas partes. Pero, si solo soy una niña, cómo iba a destrozar un pueblo yo sola. Al menos, necesitaría la ayuda de otro niño de mi edad.

–Pues que sepas que ese pueblo abandonado está lleno de fantasmas. Son los espíritus de la gente que murió allí y que se han quedado atrapados en este mundo porque hicieron cosas malas.

–¿Cosas malas? –se me escapó preguntar, aunque me había jurado que no hablaría nunca con un habitante del campo para no contagiarme.

–Sí, mataban animales para comérselos y cosas así –me contestó con un brillo muy especial en sus ojos–. No lo olvides nunca: en este pueblo ocurren sucesos muy extraños.

–¿Por la noche?

–No, qué va, en pleno día. Pero yo no te he dicho nada, que luego van por ahí los de las masias diciendo que el panadero disfruta asustando a los niños nuevos.

Y el policía, digo el panadero, se subió a su camioneta blanca de repartir el pan y se fue diciéndome adiós con la mano.

–¡¡Espero verte aquí mañana –me gritó por la ventanilla abierta mientras aceleraba–, eso querrá decir que no te has acercado al pueblo de los fantasmas!!

Un pueblo fantasma perdido en mitad del campo. Lo que faltaba: solo de verlo, a lo lejos, me daban ganas de vomitar. Era el último lugar del mundo que me gustaría visitar, aunque viviera mil años. Así que ordené a mis pies que me alejaran lo más rápido de allí.

Sin embargo, me despisté un poco siguiendo el vuelo de una mariposa azul y, sin darme cuenta... ¡¡¡zas!!! Algo muy duro me paró de golpe. Era una puerta, o mejor dicho: lo que quedaba de una puerta de madera, porque ésta cayó pulverizada a mis pies.

No me lo podía creer: sin darme cuenta, ¡¡¡¡había chocado contra la puerta de la primera casa del pueblo fantasma!!!! Grito y cortocircuito general. Mi cabeza comenzó a dar vueltas y más vueltas, sin parar, como si fuera una batidora humana, y mis piernas se iban hacia adelante y hacia atrás, a un lado y al otro, como si estuviera completamente borracha. Y todo este tembleque habría terminado muy mal, si una mano muy robusta no me hubiese cogido con fuerza del hombro.

¿Una mano? Pero... ¿no estaba en un pueblo abandonado? Los temblores de mis piernas pasaron también a mis brazos, a mis dedos, a mi cuello. ¿Acaso los fantasmas tenían manos?

–Estarás contenta –oí que alguien decía detrás de mí–: has derribado mi puerta de un solo cabezazo –lo oí o simplemente estaba soñando.

Calma. Calma. Estás en un pueblo abandonado, es decir, completamente vacío, y, que yo sepa, las paredes todavía no han aprendido a hablar. ¿O sí?... ¿No saben hablar los tarugos de mi clase?, entonces ¿por qué no podría aprender también una pared? Ya está, te tapas las orejas y... problema resuelto.

–Los chicos de ahora ya no son como los de antes. Cuando yo era joven, llamábamos a la puerta, con delicadeza, y dábamos siempre los "Buenos Días".

Menos mal que tenía las orejas tapadas, que si no, estaría muerta de miedo. Yo sabía por experiencia que los golpes en la cabeza te producían alucinaciones (como sacar un diez en mates), pero esto era demasiado.

–Niña humana, ¿me vas a ayudar a arreglar la puerta o te vas a quedar ahí parada, como si fueras una ballena en mitad del desierto?

¿Una ballena en un pueblo fantasma? Había llegado el momento de salir disparada de allí. Conté: uno... dos... y tres. Acabé tirada en una cuneta a la entrada del pueblo. ¿Por qué la gente se empeña en tirar trastos viejos en los caminos abandonados?

Primero, mis zapatillas tropezaron con tres ruedas de camión desgastadas, luego tuve que saltar una máquina de coser del año en el que inventaron la tos y, al final, tropecé con el esqueleto de una bici oxidada y caí al suelo dando una vuelta de campana.

Menos mal que en la cuneta había un colchón y no me rompí la columna de milagro. A cambio, mi cuerpo se impregnó de olor a pis de vaca.

–Pero, niña, ¿a dónde vas tan deprisa?

La voz me perseguía y eso fue peor, incluso, que el batacazo. Me puse de pie de un salto (por cierto, por una cosa de éstas en los Juegos Olímpicos te dan una medalla de oro) y me puse a correr con todas mis fuerzas.

¡¡¡Plasshhh!!! No frené hasta cerrar la puerta de mi habitación. Mi tía estaba allí limpiando no sé qué, y casi le di un susto de muerte.

–¿Qué te ha pasado, Pilar? –me preguntó tras recuperarse–, ¿has visto un fantasma?

Hasta una semana después, no pude recuperar el habla.

"Querida Pilar:

Esperamos que te lo estés pasando muy bien en el campo. Seguro que, a estas alturas, ya tienes un montón de amiguitos y sabes jugar a un montón de juegos nuevos. La gente del campo es un poco tosca, al principio, pero luego, cuando te conocen mejor, son muy generosos y te abren su corazón y ya has hecho amigos para toda la vida."

¿A quién se referirán mis padres en su último mensaje electrónico: al panadero que, en realidad, es un policía porque no para de hacer preguntas, o a los habitantes del pueblo abandonado, que, en realidad, son fantasmas?

La vida en el campo no hay quien la entienda. Parece que todo el mundo está en lo suyo y que siempre hay algo que hacer: segar la hierba, regar las plantas, podar los árboles, recoger la fruta... pero, eso es solo una tapadera para cuando les hacen fotos para los periódicos.

En realidad, los del campo solo se dedican a asustar a la gente nueva que llega de la ciudad. Te cuentan historias de brujas o de fantasmas y, la verdad, aunque seas muy valiente, te cagas de miedo. Porque en la ciudad te acostumbras a todo: atracadores de banco, asesinos de la mafia, ajustes de cuenta por lo de la droga, violadores en el parque... Lo ves en la tele y ya está, ya pasó todo, y tú estás a salvo en el comedor de tu casa, comiendo pipas y bebiendo un refresco.

En la ciudad, todo lo malo les pasa siempre a otros, que no conoces de nada, y nunca a ti. Pero en el campo es distinto. Aquí todo está cerca: las abejas, que te atacan en grupo si arrojas por un barranco su colmena, el perro pastor, que te rebana el cuello si le pegas una patada a una de sus ovejas o el agricultor, que te tira piedras si pisas su huerto de coles.

–No puedes estar todo el día encerrada en casa –me amenazó mi tía–. He hablado por teléfono con tu padre y le he pedido que venga a buscarte.

–¡¡¡Bien!!!

–Deja de dar saltos de alegría, que el suelo del primer piso es de madera y no creo que pueda aguantar más esos golpes que le das.

–Voy a preparar mi maleta.

–¡Quieta, Pilar! Tu padre no puede venir, está muy ocupado preparando no sé qué feria de la electrónica para su empresa, y me ha dicho que no puede cogerse unos días libres hasta el final del verano.

–¿Y mi madre? –pregunté.

Aunque más que una pregunta se trataba de una súplica. Mi padre era el representante de una fábrica de tuercas y tornillos y siempre tenía trabajo urgente. Como él decía, no pasaba nada si el presidente del gobierno se tomaba un mes de vacaciones, pero el mundo se podía parar de repente si faltaran tornillos y tuercas de repuesto.

–Tampoco cuentes mucho con tu madre. Tiene un congreso de no sé qué y tiene que preparar un comunicado, bien gordo, ella sola.

Los adultos siempre están igual: que si tengo mucho trabajo, que si este año no voy a tener vacaciones, que si me pagan fatal y que por eso tengo que hacer tantas horas extra. ¿Y qué pasa con los niños? ¿Es que somos muebles, que se pueden guardar en cualquier almacén, tapándolos con una sábana para que no se llenen de polvo? No me gusta el campo, pero menos aún, me gustan las personas que miden más de un metro.

–Mañana es domingo y he preparado una excursión a un lugar fantástico. Nos lo vamos a pasar tan bien, que se te van a olvidar todas tus penas.

–¿Dónde iremos, tío?, ¿a un Parque Temático?

–No, tonta, a un sitio mucho mejor.

–¡A un Centro Comercial, con hamburgueserías y cosas de esas!

–No. No das una, ¿eh Pilar?

–¿Dónde iremos, tío?

–Al pueblo abandonado, me han dicho que hay una fuente muy fresca y que, si pides un deseo...

Me desmayé, en el acto.

Al día siguiente, fuimos de excursión al pueblo de los fantasmas y mi tío, para que no me escapara, me apuntaba con su escopeta cargada. Él aseguraba que solo la llevaba para cazar algún conejo si este cometía el error de toparse con nosotros. Pero yo sabía la verdad: ¿cuántos conejos se paran en mitad de un camino abandonado para preguntarle la hora a un maldito adulto que lleva un arma cargada?

–Mira, Pilar –mi tío detuvo la marcha y se agachó para ver algo en el suelo–. Por aquí hace años que no ha pasado nadie.

No me extraña: yo siempre había preferido el campo a través. Cuando te persiguen un millón de fantasmas, uno no se para a pensar por dónde pasa el camino de regreso a casa.

–Ves, Pilar –mi tío seguía con su pesada clase de zoología–, las zarzas han invadido todo el camino y, desde aquí, prácticamente ya no se ve por dónde estaba antes la senda. ¿Has traído el machete?

Por supuesto, cómo iba a olvidarlo. Mi tío tenía su escopeta, pero yo había afilado la noche anterior el machete que me había dado para poder defenderme de los fantasmas. Esta vez no me pillarían desprevenida. Para practicar mi nueva técnica de defensa, empecé a cortar de cuajo las hierbas y enredaderas con pinchos que me iba indicando mi tío. Y así hubiera estado hasta el día del fin del mundo si, en una de las revueltas del camino, no hubiera aparecido la primera casa escondida tras los árboles.

–Ese era el molino. ¿No oyes el río cómo pasa por debajo de la casa?

Casa. ¿Qué casa? Aquello eran cuatro piedras mal colocadas.

–Aquello que ves en aquella esquina es un horno para hacer pan. Antes no había panaderías, como ahora, y cada familia tenía que hacerse sus propias hogazas. Mi abuela hacía un pan muy sabroso y duraba una semana sin ponerse duro.

¡Qué depresión me estaba entrando! Mira que tener que hacerse el pan, con lo fácil que es entrar en una pizzería y ponerte morada a pizzas.

–Vamos a verlo de cerca, te gustará –dijo mi tío metiéndose sin permiso en una de las casas que estaban a punto de venirse abajo.

–No, tío, déjalo ya, que es un poco tarde y dan una peli superguay en la tele.

–Ven, Pilar, que esto es muy bonito –se oyó como si me hablara desde el vientre de una ballena–, pero, ten cuidado, que está un poco oscuro.

Y, justo en ese momento, mi tío tocó una viga mal encajada y el techo del horno se desplomó formando una gran nube de polvo.

–¡Tío!, ¡tío!... –grité yo muerta de miedo y, entonces, oí de nuevo una voz detrás de mi espalda.

–Ya están otra vez aquí estos humanos, destrozándolo todo. No les basta con venir a vernos, tienen que destruirlo todo, son así de brutos.

–Claro, al fin y al cabo, querido, descienden del mono –le contestó otra voz menos grave.

–Querida, querrás decir de la mona, porque, que yo sepa, los monos no pueden tener hijos.

–Abuelo, abuela, ¿qué pasa? –una tercera voz, mucho más aguda, como la de un niño, sonó de pronto y se unió al coro–. Hemos oído un estruendo y hemos bajado enseguida para ver qué pasaba. ¿Es esa niña humana otra vez, abuelo?

–Sí, pero esta vez parece que viene acompañada por un adulto metomentodo.

–Querrás decir, querido, por lo que queda del adulto –le matizó la segunda voz.

Aquello era demasiado. Cualquiera podría aguantar una voz, aunque viniera del mundo de los muertos, pero tres, era demasiado. Como una máquina, empecé a excavar con las manos el montón de tierra en el que se había convertido el antiguo horno y, entre lágrima y lágrima, chillaba:

–¡Tío!, ¡tío!... ¿dónde estás? Si no estás muerto, responde por favor.

Menos mal que los viejos habitantes de aquel pueblo construían sus hornos con paja y barro que si no...

–¡Tío!, ¡tío!, si estás vivo, háblame, por favor, aunque no sea tu sobrina favorita.

Pero nadie me respondía y yo, cada segundo que pasaba, lloraba más y más y las lágrimas no me dejaban ver por dónde tenía que excavar. Además, con mis manos no avanzaba mucho, así que cogí un palo y empecé a picar con todas mis fuerzas. Y menos mal que, en ese momento, una lágrima resbaló por mi mejilla y dejó un hueco libre en mi ojo, porque estaba a punto de darle a la cabezota de mi tío con el palo.

–Tío, ¿estás bien? –nunca me había alegrado tanto de ver el careto del hermano de mi madre, y creo que nunca me alegraré tanto como en aquella ocasión.

–Abuelo, ¿le ayudamos a desenterrarlo?

Tiene gracia. El vivo, es decir, mi tío, no me hablaba y, sin embargo, los muertos (esto, los fantasmas) no paraban de darme cháchara.

–Por supuesto que no –respondió el abuelo fantasma–. Esa es la niña humana que se cargó la puerta de nuestra casa.

–¡Abuela, di algo! –protestó el pequeño fantasma.

–Venga, vejestorio, deja de hacerte el antipático –replicó la abuela fantasma–. Creo que, si la niña humana nos lo pide "por favor", bien podemos echarle una mano.

No, más manos no, que ya tuve bastante con una que me agarró ayer del hombro y me dejó helada. No obstante, la situación empezaba a ponerse tan negra (como cuando faltan dos minutos para entregar el examen de matemáticas y aún te quedan siete problemas por resolver) que no tuve más remedio que pedirles ayuda.

–Señores fantasmas –acerté a decir con un hilillo de voz–, serían tan amables de... de... ayudarme un poco.

–Todavía no he oído lo de "por favor" –contestó con frialdad el antipático del abuelo fantasma.

–Venga, querido, no seas tan quisquilloso –intervino la abuela.

–Por favor, por favor –rompí a llorar y casi inundo de agua aquel pueblo abandonado–. Mi tío se está muriendo y aquí no hay nadie que pueda ayudarme.

–¿Y nosotros no somos "nadie"?

–Abuelo, o dejas de decir tonterías o esta noche vas a dormir debajo de un castaño.

–¡Bien dicho, abuela! –concluyó el niño fantasma.

–Está bien, está bien –aceptó finalmente el abuelo fantasma–. Cantemos algo alegre y eso nos ayudará a trabajar más duro y lo sacaremos de ahí en un periquete.

Las tres voces se pusieron a cantar una canción muy rápida y, al ritmo de su canto, la tierra reseca que sepultaba el cuerpo de mi tío fue saltando por los aires, como por arte de magia, hasta desenterrarlo por completo.

–Y ahora, concluido nuestro trabajo, vamos a cantar un himno de acción de gracias.

Las voces se callaron por un momento y luego volvieron a brotar, limpias y claras, como si algún dios hubiera abierto un manantial de agua en medio del cielo. El abuelo fantasma tenía una voz oscura y grave, la abuela un poco más dulce y la del niño era tan clara y aguda, que revoloteaba por el aire como un pájaro.

Podía distinguir la voz de cada uno de ellos, pero si mi atención se alejaba, entonces, escuchaba una mezcla dulce y sin grumos, perfecta, como las natillas que hacía mi madre los domingos cuando no la habían ascendido a jefa en el trabajo y tenía tiempo para estar conmigo.

Si mis padres estuvieran aquí, seguro que no se lo creerían. Un concierto para mí sola en... un pueblo de fantasmas. Me di un par de bofetadas, lo más fuerte que pude, para averiguar si estaba dormida o... despierta.

–¡Vaya forma más rara de aplaudirnos! –el himno había terminado y la voz del abuelo volvía a resonar en mis oídos como un auténtico reproche.

–No estaba aplaudiendo, señor fantasma, solo quería estar segura de que esto no es una de mis pesadillas.

–¿Señor fantasma? –las tres voces rompieron a reír.

Y las carcajadas sonaban tan sinceras y eran tan contagiosas que, hasta a mí, me entraron ganas y acabamos todos riéndonos unos de los otros, pero de forma sana y sin malicia, todo lo contrario de lo que ocurre en el colegio. Allí todos se ríen del más débil o cuando resbalas al pisar un charco helado y se te moja hasta la ropa interior.

–Entonces, si no sois fantasmas, ¿qué sois? –me atreví a preguntarles.

La risa contagiosa es la mejor manera de hacer amigos que conozco. Una vez que te ríes con alguien, le vas cogiendo confianza y, al final, parece casi de la familia.

–Lamentamos defraudarte: no somos fantasmas.

–Y, entonces –me alarmé yo–, ¿por qué no puedo veros?

–No te asustes, es normal –me respondió con un tono muy amable la abuela–: no puedes vernos porque somos SONIDOS.

–¿Sonidos? –exclamé–. Claro, por eso no puedo veros, pero puedo oír lo que decís.

–Menos mal que vas cogiendo la idea –intervino el abuelo fantasma. Bueno, quiero decir el abuelo protestón–. Empezaba a pensar que te faltaba un tornillo en la cabeza o dos docenas, ¡quién sabe!

–Mis abuelos son dos sonidos, que un día se enamoraron y se prometieron mutuamente que siempre estarían juntos –la voz del que parecía un niño, por fin, perdió su timidez por el efecto sanador de la risa y se dispuso a contarme la historia de su familia–. Mi abuelo se llama DO –continuó–, y mi abuela RE.

–Señor DO y señora RE –hice una reverencia, pero como no estaba muy acostumbrada que digamos a hacer ese tipo de tonterías, casi me caigo de culo–. Encantada de conocerles.

–Lo mismo decimos, encantadora señorita humana.

–Eh, abuela RE, no tan deprisa, que a mí todavía no me ha pagado la puerta que destrozó el otro día.

–Como oyes, mis abuelos siempre están discutiendo, pero, en el fondo, son inseparables.

–Y tú, niño, ¿cómo te llamas? –me aventuré a preguntar.

–Me llamo SI y mis padres, MI y FA, y tengo dos hermanos: SOL y LA.

–No estoy segura del todo, pero creo que vuestros nombres me suenan de algo.

–¿Ves, antipático gruñón, como esta niña humana vale mucho? –le riñó la abuela RE a su marido.

–Nunca te acostarás sin saber una cosa más –le contestó el abuelo DO sin darle la menor importancia.

–Ya lo tengo: "Do, Re... Mi, Fa, Sol... La... y Si". ¡Sois la escala musical!

–Bueno, más bien una de ellas. Sin duda, la más conocida, al menos, por esta parte del mundo –matizó la abuela antes de que el abuelo dijese otra de sus tonterías.

–Por eso cantabais unas canciones tan bonitas, porque son una buena combinación de los sonidos de la escala musical, ¿a que sí?

–Y ya verás cuando oigas al resto de mi familia –me explicó SI. Se le notaba que se sentía un poco solo y quería ser mi amigo–. Cuando se utilizan todos los sonidos de la escala, la melodía es mucho más rica y variada

–¿Dónde está el resto?

–Mi hermano mayor, SOL, es todo un aventurero y, como no tiene miedo a nada ni a nadie, está explorando por ahí. Pero no te preocupes porque, cuando le suenan las tripas, siempre vuelve a cenar.

–Claro, solo se acuerda de su madre cuando tiene hambre, será...

–Calla, abuelo, o te dejo más solo que la una –le cortó la abuela RE.

–También tengo una hermana: LA. Es muy tímida y siempre anda escondida por ahí –continuó contándome SI–. Seguro que está oyendo todo lo que decimos, pero no sale porque te tiene miedo.

–¿Miedo? Si yo soy una niña inofensiva... –y en ese instante me arrepentí de haber traído el machete que me había dado mi tío–. Debe de ser muy bonito cuando cantáis toda la familia junta.

–Sí, antes de cada comida, cantamos siempre todos juntos para dar gracias a la naturaleza por los alimentos que nos da.

–¿Vosotros coméis? –pregunté extrañada, al fin y al cabo, eran sonidos, entes invisibles, que no tenían ni boca ni estómago.

–Mi nieto se ha expresado así para que le comprendas –me contestó la abuela RE–. Nosotros, realmente, solo nos alimentamos del aire limpio. Nos lo tragamos y después lo expulsamos y esto es lo que produce el sonido que oyes.

–Eso es lo que hago yo con mis pulmones, ¿a que sí?

–Exactamente –asintió el abuelo–. En cambio, el ruido nos puede llegar a matar. Es muy indigesto para nosotros y si, cuando tragamos el aire, nos entra mezclado con el ruido, nos ponemos fatal.

–Por eso, mi familia se ha venido a vivir al campo –me confesó mi nuevo amigo, SI–. En la ciudad, nos estábamos asfixiando.

–¡Qué historia tan triste! Lástima que no os pueda ver.

–Sí que puedes –exclamó SI con alegría–. Es decir, si quieres.

–Nada me gustaría más, pero sois sonidos y los sonidos no se ven. Es como el trino de un pájaro, es muy bonito, pero es invisible.

–Para la mayoría de la gente así ha sido a lo largo de toda la historia –me explicó con mucha paciencia la abuela RE–. En cambio, ha habido otros hombres y mujeres que sí nos han podido ver.

–¿Cómo?

–Nos han visto con una especie de disfraz, como puntos negros y blancos dibujados sobre cinco rayitas horizontales y muy finas.

–A eso le llaman las notas musicales y, a las cinco rayitas, el pentagrama –me aclaró inmediatamente SI con su habitual buen humor.

–Pero, en realidad, no somos así –me confesó con tono misterioso el abuelo DO.

–¿No?, ¿cómo sois?

–A ti te lo podemos decir, porque nos caes muy bien –me dijo al oído la abuela RE–. Los sonidos sí que pueden verse porque, aunque la gente no lo sepa, somos también... colores.

–¿Te gustaría ver cómo somos de verdad?

–Claro que sí –le respondí con la rapidez de un rayo–. Sería más que estupendo

Un enorme arco iris cayó del cielo sobre nosotros, y donde estaba la voz del abuelo DO apareció una sombra de color VERDE. La abuela RE se transformó en una bella figura AZUL y, mientras tanto, mi nuevo amigo SI se vistió de AMARILLO.

No me lo podía creer. Me froté los ojos todo lo que pude, pero allí estaban flotando a mí alrededor, mientras me hablaban, el color verde, el azul y el amarillo.Y, un poco más allá, saliendo de una casa puede ver el color VIOLETA y el MARRÓN que se acercaban hacia mí y mucho más lejos, bajando de una montaña muy alta, divisé un halo andante de color ROJO.

–¡Ah, cómo me duele la cabeza! –vaya, mi tío se estaba despertando. Me habían pasado unas cosas tan extrañas con aquella familia de sonidos, que me había olvidado por completo de que mi tío seguía ahí tumbado y completamente grogui.

–Tío, ¿estás bien? –me abalancé enseguida sobre él.

–Sí, creo que sí, si no me he roto la crisma hoy, es que no me la romperé nunca –mi tío se levantó a duras penas del suelo y se tocó, dolorido, los huesos de todo el cuerpo por si tenía algo roto–. Y tú, Pilar, ¿cómo estás?

–Muy bien, tío. Mejor que nunca. No te lo vas a creer, pero te ha salvado una familia muy especial.

–¿Aquí, en este pueblo abandonado?

–Sí, tío, ya te dije que no te lo ibas a creer.

–¿Y dónde están ahora?

–¿No les ves? –le pregunté muy extrañada–. Están aquí, junto a nosotros. Yo, al principio, pensé que eran fantasmas, porque me contó el panadero que en este pueblo abandonado pasaban cosas muy raras, pero, en realidad, son sonidos.

–¿So qué?

–Sonidos, tío. La escala musical entera, no te vayas a creer. Todavía no he conocido personalmente a todos, pero el abuelo DO, es de color verde, la abuela RE, azul, y... ¡ah!... tengo un nuevo amiguito y se llama SI.

–Y es de color rosa, ¿verdad?

–No, tío, es AMARILLO.

–Ven, Pilar, vámonos corriendo a casa. Te ha dado tanto el sol en la cabeza, que tienes una insolación y estás medio inconsciente. Pero, no te preocupes, que eso se cura con un par de pastillas que nos dará el médico de cabecera. Seguro que dejas de ver colores extraños y de decir bobadas.

Mi tío me cogió en brazos y no me soltó hasta que llegamos a la consulta del doctor más cercano, que estaba a más de cincuenta kilómetros de curvas y más curvas. Cuando llegué, estaba tan mareada por el viaje en coche a todo trapo (mi tío estaba realmente preocupado por mi salud), que, al ver la bata blanca del médico, vomité en ella todo lo que había comido durante la última semana.

–Ya lo ve, doctor –trató de disculparse mi tío–, esta niña está muy enferma y dice cosas muy raras.

¡¡¡Milagro!!! A la mañana siguiente ya estaba bien.

–¡Qué!, estás pensando en visitar el pueblo abandonado, ¿a que sí? –me preguntó el panadero–policía al verme de nuevo.

–No, qué va.

–¡Ni se te ocurra! Allí ocurren cosas terribles –bramó mientras me daba el pan–. Si entras en ese pueblo maldito, no podrás volver a salir nunca más.

¡Ja, ja!, a mí los pueblos fantasmas ya no me asustan. Soy una niña de ciudad, o sea, muy poco impresionable. Dejé las tres barras en la mesa de la cocina y, media hora después, pasaba por delante de la primera casa abandonada. El abuelo DO ya había arreglado la puerta y esta incluso parecía mucho más nueva que cuando la derribé, sin querer, de un cabezazo.

Luego, andando de puntas para no hacer ruido, me acerqué al horno (o lo que quedaba de él tras la visita arrasadora de mi tío) y vi que SI me estaba esperando silbando una hermosa melodía.

–Sabía que regresarías –soltó al verme y sin dejar de silbar–. Mi abuelo, en cambio, apostó un barril de cerveza a que todavía estarías corriendo del susto que te dimos y que, a estas alturas, sobrepasarías Groenlandia.

–Me alegro de que el simpático de tu abuelo haya perdido la apuesta –le contesté con cierta maldad.

–Aún no cantes victoria: el abuelo es muy mal pagador y seguro que nos da largas, hasta que ya nadie se acuerde de la apuesta.

Mi nuevo amigo, SI, no estaba solo. Junto a él había una figura delgada, de color naranja, que me miraba, de arriba abajo, con mucho descaro.

–¡Ah!... Esta es mi hermana pequeña y se llama LA. Es un poco revoltosa, pero tiene buen corazón.

–¡Hola, LA! –la saludé levantando la mano y la pequeña salió disparada para esconderse detrás de un árbol seco que había en medio de la plaza del pueblo.

–No te preocupes, LA es así de rara. Está enfadada desde que vinimos a vivir al campo.

–La entiendo perfectamente –le contesté con conocimiento de causa–. En la ciudad hay muchas comodidades.

–Tal vez para los humanos, pero nosotros, los sonidos, somos diferentes.

–¿Por qué? –quise saber llena de curiosidad.

–El ruido nos mata y en las ciudades cada vez hay más. Los atascos de los coches cada día son más grandes, en los bares ponen la música a todo volumen y hay miles de máquinas excavadoras haciendo agujeros por las calles para arreglar nadie sabe exactamente qué.

–Para de contar, por favor, que me estás dando dolor de cabeza.

–¿Ves cómo tengo razón? En la ciudad, con tanto ruido por cualquier sitio ya no podemos respirar y nos ahogamos.

–¡Qué pena, con lo bien que cantáis! –me quejé–. Vuestras voces me recuerdan al canto de los pájaros en los parques y...

–¿Todavía quedan pájaros en vuestras ciudades llenas de ruidos insoportables? –se extrañó SI.

–Bueno, muchos se han ido ya, por lo del ruido y la contaminación, ya sabes.

–A mis abuelos también les pasó lo mismo: tuvieron que marcharse para poder sobrevivir. Vivían cerca de un aeropuerto y los aviones despegaban o aterrizaban cada 3 minutos y no les dejaban dormir.

–Aquí en el campo estaréis bien –accedí a decir tras pensar, por primera vez en mi vida, en los inconvenientes de la vida en la ciudad–. El aire huele a limpio y, como el pueblo está abandonado, no hay excavadoras, ni coches, ni camiones de la basura, ni aviones que os molesten.

–Además –añadió SI–, aquí estamos en contacto con nuestros antepasados más directos.

–¿Los monos? –dije volviendo a meter la pata hasta el fondo.

–No, tonta, los sonidos de la naturaleza: el piar de los pájaros, el gorgoteo del agua al precipitarse entre las rocas de los riachuelos, el murmullo de las hojas cuando las mece el viento, el crujir de los grillos por la noche...

–¿Y eso no son también ruidos?

–No, amiga, no los confundas con tu mente de urbanita. Eso son sonidos, porque cuando los oyes no te molestan ni te ponen nervioso, como el frenazo de un autobús. Todo lo contrario, te transmiten paz interior y armonía.

–¡Ah!... es verdad, no lo había pensado antes.

–¡Qué divertido!, pero ¿cómo funciona?

–Es muy fácil, los humanos siempre han construido instrumentos para tratar de imitar los sonidos del agua, el lenguaje de los pájaros o el retumbar de los relámpagos en las tormentas. Primero fabricaron toscos tambores con la piel de los animales que cazaban, después pequeñas flautas con las ramas secas de los árboles y, por último, han llegado a crear la máquina más perfecta de hacer sonidos: la orquesta.

–Yo tengo un primo lejano que toca el violín en una de ellas y se lo pasa genial –me dí cuenta de repente–. Quizá debería hacerle una visita...

–Sí, la música es muy divertida y seguro que si le oyes tocar, te lo pasarás muy bien. Y, por cierto, ¿a ti no te afecta el ruido y la contaminación de las ciudades?

–¡Qué va! –le contesté haciéndome la valiente–. Mis orejas y mis pulmones están acostumbrados. Es más. Cuando llegué aquí, casi me da un patatús al respirar tanto aire limpio de una vez.

LA, que lo oía todo desde su escondrijo del árbol, no pudo reprimir su risa y, casi sin darse cuenta, volvió a acercarse a nosotros.

–Parece un angelito, pero seguro que está tramando algo –me advirtió SI entre carcajada y carcajada.

–LA, ¿te gusta vivir en el campo? –le pregunté tratando de ser amable.

–¡No! –me contestó sin dudarlo. Tenía la segunda voz más aguda de toda la familia.

–¿Y a ti te gustaría aprender música? –contraatacó su hermano–. Así podríamos cantar todos juntos y nos divertiríamos mucho.

–¡Oh, no!, mis amigos dicen que estudiar música es muy aburrido.

–¿Aburrido?

–Sí, en el colegio tenemos dos clases a la semana y la profe nos obliga a leer un libro que está lleno de dibujitos muy raros. Creo que se llaman corcheas, claves y… cazuelas.

–Cazuelas, no, "calderones", querrás decir –me corrigió LA riéndose de mí otra vez.

–Sí, eso, "calderones"... es que, con tantas palabrotas raras que hay en la música, se me amontonan en la lengua y, al final, me atasco.

–Mira, mi hermana es muy pequeña y ya sabe música.

–¿De verdad? –pregunté yo realmente maravillada–. Igual es un genio, como Mozart.

–Mi abuelo, que es muy viejo, conoció personalmente a Mozart y este le confesó que todo el mundo podía disfrutar de la música tanto como él.

–¿Que tu abuelo conoció a Mozart? ¡eso es imposible! –concluí algo molesta.

–Claro, los sonidos somos inmortales, como la misma música, ¿o acaso tú no has oído alguna vez una pieza musical de Mozart?

–Creo que sí, una vez que fui al dentista y la ponían para calmar los nervios a los pacientes.

–Pues, niña sabelotodo, esa música fue compuesta hace más de 200 años y ahí la tienes, tan fresca como el primer día.

–¡No estamos hablando de lo mismo!

"¿Te gustaría aprender música?" La preguntita parecía ingenua, pero seguía retumbando dentro de mi cabeza como una pelota de ping-pong en pleno partido entre dos chinos. Y digo yo: ¿quién quiere aprender esas melodías para imbéciles que salen en los anuncios de la tele? "¡Compre en los Supermercados Estafador! (Pim, pam, ping,dong), los únicos que merecen su atención!" (Lari, laró, lari, laré) ¡Música! ¡¡Música!! ¡¡¡MÚSICA!!!

Igual que el humo supernegro que echan los tubos de escape de los coches, está en todas partes. En las pelis, en la cola de la panadería, en la consulta del pediatra, en el andén del metro ("Atención, por favor, por una avería en la línea 6, los trenes circulan con un retraso de dos horas, perdonen las molestias") Puaff, ¿a quién le gusta ese soniquete zumbón?

¿Y qué me dices de las clases de música del colegio? Primero tienes que comprar una flauta de plástico malo que se te pega en los dedos y que huele fatal y eso es solo el principio. Después viene el tiro de gracia, te obligan a soplar por ese artefacto inmundo durante horas y horas y ¿qué consigues a cambio?: un chirrido horripilante que es capaz de ahuyentar hasta los vampiros. ¿Has probado alguna vez pisar el rabo de tu gato con todas tus fuerzas cuando duerme junto al radiador? Pues la flauta del cole suena igual. ¡Música! ¡Vaya tostón!

–¿No te gusta la música? –insistió SI al ver la cara de asco que estaba poniendo.

–¿Acaso te crees que soy una niña idiota? –le contesté a bocajarro.

–No seas terca, pequeña amiga –la abuela RE, vestida con un bonito traje de terciopelo azul, acababa de asomarse al balcón de su casa y me miraba con la cara que ponen los adultos cuando te van a echar un sermón–. Todo el mundo puede aprender y disfrutar con la música.

–Todos no –volví yo a la carga–. En mi colegio, nadie presta atención a lo que nos explica la profe de música porque es un tostón.

–Abuela, ya te dije yo que esta niña humana era como el resto de su especie: unos imbéciles con orejas.

–Abuelo DO, siempre andas metiendo la pata donde nadie te llama –le gritó la abuela desde el balcón, y el abuelo volvió a meter su cabezota por la misma ventana por donde la había sacado unos segundos antes.

–No le hagas caso, niña, es un gruñón maleducado.

–Abuela, ¿por qué no le cuentas algo sobre la música, a ver si cambia de opinión? –intervino SI en mi defensa.

–Está bien, esperadme ahí, que ahora bajo.

Se oyeron unos pasos en el interior de la casa y la abuela apareció llevando un libro muy fino. Bueno, más bien habría que decir que el libro se llevaba a sí mismo, porque iba flotando, dulcemente, al lado de RE y sin despegarse apenas de su figura azul.

–Niños, vamos a sentarnos debajo de aquel castaño centenario –sugirió la abuela, pero yo tuve que estropearlo otra vez.

–Hace mucho calor, ¿por qué no entramos dentro de la casa y ponemos el aire acondicionado?

–Creo que has vuelto a mear fuera del tiesto –el abuelo me riñó, otra vez, desde dentro de la casa.

–La brisa y la sombra fresca de las hojas de los árboles son el mejor aire acondicionado que existe –trató la abuela de calmarme–.

Además, este sistema no consume electricidad y, por lo tanto, tampoco contamina.

Con la lección aprendida, me senté debajo de un castaño del tamaño de un rascacielos y, aunque al principio me pinché las piernas con la hierba seca, a los dos minutos me sentía más cómoda que en el sillón favorito de mi casa.

–¿Estáis listos? –los tres muchachos asentimos y la abuela abrió el libro que le había acompañado hasta allí.

–Este libro de música me gusta más que el mío: es menos grueso.

–Mira y calla, que las niñas de ciudad no sabéis ni ver ni escuchar.

–¿De verdad quieres aprender música?

La hermana de SI me miró como si nunca hubiera visto antes un ser humano.

En la cena, esa noche, nadie se movía. Mi tío miraba a mi tía y mi tía el cactus que malvivía olvidado en un rincón del comedor lleno de moho. Yo, a esa hora, ya habría derramado tres veces mi vaso de leche, utilizado mi cuchara como catapulta para lanzar mis guisantes al jardín (¡odio el verde!, no sé si este punto ha quedado del todo claro) y mi camisa estaría ya perdida de lamparones de puré de patatas. Sin embargo, aquella noche todo era diferente. El nuevo y único huésped de mi tío iba a bajar a cenar y el silencio era absoluto. Solo los ojos del hermano de mi madre se movían de un lado para otro, como si temieran la aparición de un monstruo.

–¿Va a bajar o no? –por fin mi tía se atrevió a hablar, porque la sopa se estaba quedando al gusto de los pingüinos del Polo Sur.

–No sé –respondió mi tío con una sonrisa más petrificada que los muslos de pollo al limón, que se pudrían desde hacía tiempo en una bandeja cursi con dibujos de patos y cañas de bambú.

–¿Qué te dijo?

–No sé –volvió a repetir el hermano de mi madre. Creo que sus neuronas se estaban disecando a la misma velocidad de los cohetes que viajan a la Luna.

–¡¿Cómo que no lo sabes?! Tú eres el dueño de esta casa rural y él es tu cliente. Tu único cliente en 20 años. Tú... tienes... que... saber... si viene a cenar o no, porque, no sé si recuerdas, me has ordenado esta mañana que prepare comida para diez.

–Es que algo me dice que come como un tiburón.

Al oír la palabra "tiburón" todos nos quedamos de nuevo en silencio y, entonces, solo entonces, pudimos oír un silbido muy estridente que nos llegaba desde el piso de arriba.

–¿Te has dejado encendida la tele de nuestro cuarto, cariño? –preguntó mi tía extrañada.

–No, no funciona desde que le tire mis zapatillas deportivas a ese invitado de "Tarta rosa", el primo ese del marqués de no sé qué, que no paraba de llamarnos "rurales" a los que vivimos en el campo.

"Tarta Rosa" (no hace falta decirlo) es ese programa de televisión tan instructivo donde van los conductores, secretarias, canguros y limpiadoras de los famosos a despellejar a sus amos a cambio de un buen fajo de billetes.

–¿Y, si la tele está estropeada, quién está silbando? –volvió a preguntar mi tía con más asco que curiosidad.

La cancioncilla, en cuestión, era realmente horrorosa y, cada vez, sonaba más cerca de nuestro pescuezo sin que nadie en la mesa se atreviera a mirar de dónde venía.

–¿Qué tal familia?

La musiquilla paró en seco y una voz muy chillona nos perforó el tímpano. Era la voz más desagradable que había oído nunca. Me tapé enseguida las orejas con mi servilleta, pero el truco no funcionó.

–¿Ah, es usted? –mi tío se levantó de la mesa con muy pocas ganas y le estrechó la mano a esa voz chillona con patas.

Mi tío había confundido esa cosa que teníamos delante con un tiburón, pero a mí, en cambio, me parecía más un extraterrestre. Atención. Tenía la cabeza gorda y redonda, como un garbanzo gigante, y, en cambio, un cuerpo más delgado que el poste de un semáforo. Con esos atributos físicos, más que andar moviendo los pies, era su cráneo (totalmente pelado) el que se desplazaba de un lado para otro, como si se le fuera a caer del peso que tenía. Una cerilla gigante no tendría mejor pinta que aquel ser de otra galaxia.

Aunque, eso sí, iba vestido con elegancia: un traje de chaqueta blanco, con su pajarita negra a juego. En resumen, era un cabezón... multimillonario.

–Gracias por su amable recibimiento –continuó hablando el huésped de mi tío–, y no dejen de cenar, que yo me apaño con cualquier cosa que haya en la nevera.

¿Comer, con "aquello" delante de tus narices? Imposible. A mí se me había ido el apetito para siempre jamás. Tan asqueroso era aquel ser de otro planeta que me entraron unas ganas enormes de vomitar. Cada vez que abría la boca, una lengua, delgada y muy roja, luchaba por salir y nos salpicaba a todos de saliva amarillenta. Para defenderme de su ataque salival, yo maniobré para lanzarle mi plato de sopa directamente a la cara del alienígena, pero mi tía adivinó mis intenciones y me desactivó con una de sus famosas miradas paralizantes.

–Siéntese, por favor –le aconsejó mi tío después de chocarle la mano y restregársela disimuladamente para limpiar las gotas de saliva que le habían caído.

La criatura de otro mundo se paró frente a mí y me miró, de arriba abajo, con sus ojos de koala que sin duda servían también para ver por dentro de mi cuerpo. Ser extraterrestre tenía que tener alguna ventaja, digo yo.

–Niña, ¿se te ha comido la lengua el gato? –hablando de animales de compañía, si las ratas de cloaca hablaran, su voz sería sin duda alguna mucho más agradable que la de ese fósforo andante.

–No le haga caso, es una niña de ciudad –intervino mi tía en mi defensa–, y ya se sabe, allí no les enseñan buenos modales en la escuela.

Por una vez mi tía tenía razón. Los buenos modales no son nada prácticos. Si una niña no sabe decir tacos, cómo se va a defender cuando un coche intente atropellarla en un paso de cebra.

–¿Quiere un poco de pollo? –intervino mi tío ofreciéndole la fuente.

–Sí, gracias, el campo me abre un apetito de lobo.

El ente se sentó de un saltito en la única silla que quedaba libre. Me arrepentí de no haberme dejado olvidadas siete chinchetas donde había aterrizado su culo de otro planeta.

Sin darse cuenta de mis verdaderas intenciones, el extraterrestre me sonrió, me roció con una buena ración de sus fluidos salivares y se puso a masticar y a escupir a toda máquina. Ahora entendía lo del hambre canina. Sus manos, blancas y sin pelos, destrozaban el pan y, entre bocado y bocado, las migajas huían despavoridas al ver que un monstruo de dientes enormes trataba de engullirlas. A mí, por mucho menos que eso, mi padre me hubiera castigado una semana sin postre.

–¿Está de vacaciones? –quiso saber mi tío.

Ante todo pretendía ser amable, porque el último cliente que pasó una noche en la casa rural no quiso volver nunca más. Dijo que un mosquito había entrado por la ventana de su cuarto y que no pudo dormir el resto de la noche del miedo que tenía a morir desangrado.

–No, qué va. Yo nunca tengo vacaciones –le respondió el extraterrestre. Bueno, en eso se parece a muchos habitantes de la Tierra–. Odio estar sin hacer nada. Me gusta la actividad: coger el coche para ir a trabajar, aparcar en doble fila, comer en buenos restaurantes, ir de compras, subir y bajar escaleras mecánicas... vaya, lo normal. No me gusta estar parado, me oxido.

De pronto, volvió a sonar la musiquilla estúpida del principio y, con un tic nervioso, el ente comenzó a tocarse todo su cuerpo, hasta que la melodía se hizo insoportable y sus tentáculos lograron sacar de uno de sus bolsillos un teléfono móvil repleto de lucecitas verdosas.

–Disculpen un momento –silbó con su lengüecita de reptil y se puso el aparatejo a la altura de su boquita de pitiminí–. ¡He ordenado que no se me moleste bajo ningún concepto! –gritó antes

de que su interlocutor pudiera decir "hola"– ¡¿Está suficientemente claro?!... Hasta nunca –y apagó el móvil con cara de asco.

–¿Algún problema? –se interesó mi tío que, por ese tipo de intervenciones, tenía bien ganada la fama de bocazas.

–No, ninguno que no se pueda resolver con un par de órdenes bien formuladas –tras esconder de nuevo el teléfono en su elegante chaqueta de lino, el extraterrestre volvió a engullir sus mulos de pollo con las mismas ganas que sus congéneres debían invadir los planetas de otra galaxia–. Estoy acostumbrado. A las personas imprescindibles nos llaman continuamente por teléfono. La gente, ya se sabe, no puede vivir sin nosotros.

–Ya... –le cortó mi tía con ganas de irse a la cama para no tener que aguantar más a ese vanidoso–. Los hombres de negocios ya se sabe...

–Mucho me temo que se equivoca usted, señora. Yo me dedico a la música. Soy compositor.

–Perdone, usted, pero con ese traje tan caro le confundí con un ejecutivo de alguna gran multinacional.

–Me halaga, señora mía –reconoció el ente cabezón, exhibiendo una amplia sonrisa de satisfacción que originó una nueva lluvia de saliva a su alrededor–. Aunque, he de reconocer, que la música también es un negocio.

–¿Cómo dice? –a mi tío se le atragantó un hueso de pollo en la epiglotis–. ¿Puede repetir eso último, por favor?

–Por supuesto, querido amigo. LA MÚSICA ES... UN NEGOCIO.

–Me parece que no le entiendo –mi tío desde pequeño había sido el tonto de la familia.

–Déjeme que se lo explique –el extraterrestre se levantó de un salto y se puso a gesticular como un payaso en la pista del circo–. "Mira, mira a tu vecina" –arrancó a cantar con su voz atildada–. "Ella es más lista, ella es más bella, porque compra siempre en los supermercados LA ESTRELLA". Seguro que se acuerdan de esta cancioncilla tan pegadiza, ¿verdad? La compuse yo mismo y... a la gente, al oírla a todas horas por radio y televisión, le entraron unas ganas locas de comprar y vaciaron todas las estanterías del supermercado. Y eso que sus productos eran mucho más caros...

Aprovechando que acababa de entrar en estado de éxtasis, quise propinarle una patada en el culo, pero el brazo de mi tía me retuvo en la silla. Mi tío, el muy tonto, se puso a aplaudir la actuación del fósforo andante, mientras este se secaba el sudor de su cabezota con cuatro servilletas: la suya... y las nuestras.

–Esa melodía se me ocurrió en apenas un par de minutos... y con ella he ganado montones de dinero. Era tan contagiosa como la gripe en el vagón de un tren, todo el mundo la tatareaba, la silbaba, la cantaba... en el ascensor, en los pasillos del metro, en la ducha... y después de ese éxito, vinieron muchos otros: "Mantequilla La Mugre", "Bragas Tapalotodo"...

–Así que es usted músico –metió baza mi tía en un intento desesperado por acabar con aquel culebrón.

–Algo más que eso. Mozart y Beethoven, por citar algunos casos, crearon piezas inmortales, pero yo he ido mucho más allá: me he forrado. Mis melodías son tan pegadizas, que la gente se cree todo lo que cuentan. Con decirle que, debido al éxito de ventas, los supermercados "La Estrella" tuvieron que cambiar de nombre. Ahora se llaman "Supermercados La Galaxia".

–Es el negocio del siglo: todo beneficios y ningún riesgo.

–Así es, amigo mío. Todo era perfecto... hasta que un día perdí la inspiración.

El ente cabezón se echó a llorar y los mocos rodaron por el mantel formando una cascada nauseabunda.

Domingo por la mañana, muy temprano. ¿Hay algo más inocente que una niña jugando en el césped... pisando los geranios, destrozando las fresas que iban destinadas a la tarta dominical o derribando un par de macetas con rosas blancas y amarillas, de esas que las mujeres del campo suelen presentar a los concursos florales para llevarse el primer premio y ser la envidia de sus vecinas?

Todo era perfecto: el cielo estaba azul, los pájaros trinaban en las ramas de los árboles, un viento suave mecía las hojas, un cabezón se acercaba en traje de baño, una paloma blanca bebía en la fuente con forma de concha marina, las campanas repicaban en el fondo del valle, las cumbres nevadas... ¡un momento, un momento...! ¡¿qué hace un cabezón aquí estropeándome el cuadro?!

–Hola, pequeña –me lo temía: lo del cabezón no era ningún invento, era tan real como la vida misma–. Perdona... creo que anoche, con la prisas, no me acordé de presentarme. Me llamo Pelayo García Ansuátegui. Los demás adultos me llaman "don Pelayo", pero, como me has caído muy simpática, hasta que cumplas los 15 te dejo que me llames simplemente "PGA". Es mucho más corto y así seguro que te acuerdas antes, ¿a que sí cielo?

¡Puaff...!, qué babosos se ponen los mayores cuando te van a pedir algo.

–Y ahora que somos amigos, ¿te gustaría ayudarme a encontrar algo muy importante que he perdido?

¿No te lo dije? Si es que se les ve venir cuando ponen cara de tonto y empiezan a hablar muy despacio.

–He de confesarte una cosa muy importante, pero con la condición de que no se la cuentes a nadie. A nadie, ¿has entendido?, ni siquiera a tu madre o... a tu padre.

¿Cómo se lo iba a contar si estaban a 600 kilómetros de distancia? Los adultos son realmente estúpidos. Y don Pelayo (es decir, PGA) se disponía a batir un nuevo record mundial.

–Mira, seguro que te estarás preguntando por qué me he levantado tan temprano.

–Porque le han despertado los puñeteros pájaros. Hay que ver el ruido que montan a las seis de la mañana.

–Oye, se nota que eres una niña muy inteligente y despierta –al extraterrestre cabezón le entró un ataque de hipo–. Pero no hables tan alto, que despiertas a toda la casa y eso es lo último que necesitamos. Mira, pequeña, he perdido la inspiración y no puedo ni dormir.

–¿Y eso no se puede comprar en el supermercado? –le pregunté, un tanto harta ya de este jueguecito de preguntas y respuestas.

–Me temo que no. En música, la inspiración son unos duendecillos verdes que viven en los bosques y que, cuando te duermes, si has sido bueno, te susurran melodías inmortales.

¿Duendes verdes? Don Pelayo estaba mucho peor de lo que creía. Los mayores nunca dejan de sorprenderte, aunque estés jugando en el césped a las seis de la mañana y haga un frío que pela.

–Por esa razón, he venido al campo –prosiguió el cabezón sin darle la menor importancia a la cara de póker que le había puesto–, porque en la ciudad ya han talado todos los árboles que había para hacer autopistas, y los duendes se han ido para siempre.

–Ahhhh, ya lo entiendo –caí por fin en la cuenta–, por eso los gitanos dicen que cuando cantas muy bien tienes "duende".

–Perfecto, perfecto, me alegra comprobar que has cogido la idea. Yo leí de pequeño que a los duendes les gusta jugar en las praderas que hay junto a los riachuelos de aguas limpias. Aquí seguro que hay cosas de esas, ¿verdad?

–No sé –le contesté arrancando una margarita.

–No te hagas la loca, niña. Sé perfectamente que todos los niños del mundo creen en la existencia de estos seres mágicos... y tú no vas a ser una excepción.

La paloma blanca se echó a volar (bueno, he de reconocer que le lancé una piedra, pero pequeñita, pequeñita) y, como acto de venganza, bombardeó la calva de don Pelayo con un par de cagarrutas.

–Niña, por favor, no te distraigas. A la gente normal le daría un patatús si viera a una de estas criaturillas diminutas y juguetonas, de nariz larga y orejas puntiagudas. Solo los grandes compositores de música, como yo, estamos acostumbrados a su presencia.

–Y, si les conoce tanto, ¿por qué ya no le susurran música?

–Ya te lo he dicho: han huído de las ciudades –PGA comenzó a mosquearse conmigo no sé aún por qué–. Ya no hay árboles donde puedan vivir y, además, el ruido les mata. El ruido es el peor veneno que puede existir para un duende de la música. Lo temen más que a los gatos. Y en las grandes ciudades hay ya más coches que gatos, ¿me entiendes o no?

¡Vaya tontería! A mí me encanta el ruido. Cuanto más, mejor. Es más, si de repente todos los coches, los autobuses, los camiones de la basura, las máquinas perforadoras, los altavoces de todos los bares del mundo... se parasen, puafff... el silencio sería... insoportable.

–Odio los mosquitos, pero necesito encontrar un par de duendecillos del bosque. ¿Me ayudarás, niña buena? –me rogó don Pelayo poniéndose de rodillas.

–¿Y qué hará con ellos cuando los encontremos?

–Los cazaré, como si fueran zorros, y los pondré dentro de una jaula de acero para que no puedan escaparse nunca más. Y cuando llegue la noche y todo el mundo se haya ido a dormir, los sacaré del armario y les obligaré a que me susurren al oído las más bellas melodías del universo. ¡Me haré multimillonario, sí señor! Y a ti, por tu ayuda, te haré un gran regalo. ¿Qué te parece una bolsita de chucherías?

Don Pelayo era un hombre de palabra. Inmediatamente se puso a buscar debajo de las macetas de mi tía, dentro de los setos que separaban la finca de mi tío y, como no encontraba nada, hasta se atrevió a meter sus delicados dedos en un montón de estiércol de oveja que usaban para abonar las matas de tomates. Y esto último se lo tomó con mucha calma y precisión. Sacó una lupa y mi tío casi lo atropella con su carretilla de llevar el pienso a las vacas del establo.

–¡Don Pelayo, pero qué hace aquí tan temprano! – y no era fácil reconocerle porque, como consecuencia del golpe con la carretilla, su cabezota se había incrustado de lleno en el estiércol–. Si sigue ahí quieto se va a congelar.

Como siempre, el consejo de mi tío llegaba tarde. El cuerpo descompensado de Don Pelayo estaba ya tan congelado como esos astronautas que piensan crionizar para que resistan el viaje a Marte.

–Cariño, sal de la cocina, esto es una emergencia –se desesperó mi tío al ver el pastel. ¡Bah!... los mayores se alarman por cualquier cosa.

–¿A quién se le ocurre salir en bañador al jardín tan temprano y con el frío que hace? –le riñó mi tía–. Querido, ¿no te he dicho mil veces que adviertas a tus clientes que esto es la montaña, que estamos a más de 2.000 metros de altura y que aquí no hace tanto calor como en la playa?

–Ahora que lo dices, creo que me olvidé de mencionarlo.

Menos mal que, dos horas después, el sol comenzó a brillar en el horizonte y don Pelayo fue descongelándose poco a poco, como el filete de merluza que mi madre me pone para cenar todos los viernes.

Don Pelayo estaba completamente loco, pero esto lo hacía mucho más interesante que el resto de los adultos. Durante una semana, estuvo buscando por los alrededores a sus duendecillos mágicos y musicales, y... se cayó tres veces al río, se fracturó una costilla al caer desde lo alto de un roble centenario y le picaron en el culo todas, y cada una, de las abejas de un panel que confundió con una cabina pública de teléfono.

Cargado con sus prismáticos de visión nocturna y una lupa, nos decía que salía a buscar setas, pero, cuando regresaba por la noche, tenía la calva abollada y el cuerpo lleno de pinchos como si le hubiera pasado por encima una manada de búfalos cabreados.

–¿Coger setas en pleno verano?

–Eso dice, querida –se lavaba las manos mi tío. Todas las noches le subía a su habitación una caja de calmantes y, aún así, los alaridos de dolor de PGA se podían oír a diez kilómetros a la redonda.

Aquello no podía continuar así. Sus "ayayays" no me dejaban dormir y no me quedó más remedio que ayudarle. Aunque, he de reconocer, que la copa de helado de tres sabores que me regaló, también influyó un poco en mi decisión.

–Niña, seguro que tú sabes dónde viven los duendes de la música, ¿a que sí? –me interrogaba cada noche PGA entre dolor y dolor–.

Más, menudo dilema se me presentaba: ¿cómo podía ayudar a don Pelayo (y lo más importante: seguir comiendo un helado gratis todas las tardes) sin traicionar a mis nuevos y tan especiales amigos, que vivían en el pueblo abandonado?

Le di muchas vueltas y, por fin, encontré la solución. Ayudaría a don Pelayo, pero en la dirección contraria.

El primer día le envié directamente a una cueva... y resultó que estaba llena de serpientes hambrientas. Esa noche al ente barrigón le subió tanto la fiebre que el termómetro le estalló nada más ser introducido en su boca. Mi tía insistió en llamar al médico de guardia, pero mi tío tenía alergia a los matasanos y, al final, lo curó del todo con un par de píldoras... para las diarreas de los caballos.

El segundo día me disculpé y le dije que ahora lo recordaba todo, que los duendecillos de la música vivían en un laberinto subterráneo rodeados de platos de oro y diamantes. Le señalé un punto al lado de la carretera y, sin preguntarme nada, se puso a cavar y picar, hasta que reventó la tubería que conectaba todos los retretes del pueblo y le sepultó una avalancha de pis y caca.

–Oh... lo siento –intenté disculparme, sin poder contener la risa al verle convertido en el "hombre-excremento".

–Bueno, niña, un pequeño error de cálculo lo comete hasta el científico más famoso.

Como podéis comprobar, tampoco esa vez se desanimó y volvió a implorarme que le dijera dónde estaba el escondite secreto de los Duendes de la Música.

–Si me lo pides de rodillas, quizá... –le contesté toda seria por fuera, aunque por dentro me seguía muriendo de risa.

El compositor egoísta se arrodilló y yo, con la dignidad de una princesa cursi, le susurré algo al oído. Saltó a la velocidad de la luz y se fue corriendo después de caerse un montón de veces. Tres horas más tarde, una cuadrilla de cortadores de leña lo trajeron resoplando y acordándose de toda mi familia. Estaba tan gordo que se quedó atascado, cuando intentó entrar por un agujero enorme que un rayo maleducado abrió en un árbol centenario y que, desde entonces, se había convertido en una colonia de vacaciones para las arañas del entorno.

Al día siguiente, PGA no bajó a desayunar.

–Don Pelayo se ha vuelto de repente muy deportista, querida –se extrañó mi tío cuando nos sentábamos a la mesa ante un buen tazón de leche recién ordeñada. ¡Vaya asco, no tenía cacao!

–¿Lo dices por las moraduras que tiene por todo el cuerpo? –le contestó su mujer con ironía.

–No, me ha dicho que no volverá hasta mañana, porque se va a la capital a ver un partido de fútbol, la final de no sé qué.

Vaya, me quedé sin diversión. Para una vez que encuentro a un adulto que hace caso a lo que le dicen los niños... Sin mi nuevo juguete, la jornada se presentaba muy aburrida, así que decidí hacerles una visita a mis amigos del pueblo abandonado.

Como de costumbre, me lancé rodando por una pradera verde aplastando flores amarillas, trepé a un par de árboles (por si había algún nido de urracas con anillos de oro) y tiré piedras a las colmenas para cabrear un poco a las abejas. Hice el humano un par de horas (antes se decía hacer el animal) y el olorcillo a queso rancio seguía allí, pegado a mi nariz. Además, de vez en cuando, oía un "ayayay", que me era familiar, y otras un "me cago en esta niña del demonio", pero me volvía rápidamente y detrás de mí no veía nunca a nadie. Así que decidí no darle la menor importancia a estos pequeños detalles.

Por fin me acerqué a las casas en ruina y SI me saludó desde una de las ventanas.

–¿Has venido a tu clase de música?

–¿Tú que crees? Si fuera de mates, estaría a mil años luz de aquí.

–Ahora bajo.

En un pispás, SI apareció junto a mí. Ser un sonido tenía estas ventajillas: si te tirabas de un décimo piso, no te partías el espinazo, ni te salía una buena colección de chichones.

–Al fin veo una cara amiga –abrí la boca para disipar mis propios pensamientos negativos.

–Espero que no te haya seguido nadie hasta aquí –me advirtió SI mostrándome su cara más seria–.

–No te preocupes. Hay un pedante preguntón hospedado en la casa de mis tíos, pero seguro que, a estas horas, ya se estará arrepintiendo de haberme preguntado dónde os podía encontrar.

–Menos mal que eres una niña inteligente. Hoy es un día crítico. Mi padre es alérgico a los madrugones (nunca se levanta antes de las doce) y hoy, como es su turno, no hay nadie vigilando.

–¡Abuela, la humana ya está aquí… molestando!

La pequeña LA volvió a berrear desde alguno de sus escondites secretos y a mí me hubiera gustado darle los buenos días, personalmente, para poder estrujarle la epiglotis.

–Perdona a mi hermana, no le gustan nada los extraños.

–Yo no soy una extraña –me defendí cada vez más enfadada–. Soy una niña de ciudad y todos los niños de ciudad somos iguales en cualquier lugar del mundo. Por ejemplo, nos gustan las mismas cosas: pisar las flores del parque, tirar los papeles al suelo, inundar los hormigueros, romper las ramas de los árboles…

–Vale, vale –me cortó SI–. Nosotros, los sonidos musicales, somos diferentes.

–¿No me digas que sois una familia de piratas y tenéis una isla, con su tesoro y todo?

–No, qué va. Los humanos siempre estáis pensando en el dinero. Para nosotros, no tiene ningún valor. Lo importante es vivir en armonía con la naturaleza.

–Al principio todo iba bien –continuó la madre–. Los humanos soplaban o acariciaban con delicadeza sus instrumentos y nosotros, los sonidos, salíamos al exterior cantando alegres melodías, como en un día de fiesta.

–¡Qué calentito se vivía dentro de un viejo contrabajo! –aulló el abuelo DO saliendo de quién sabe dónde.

–Yo prefería las flautas dulces. Su sonido era el preferido en los salones de la gente elegante y, después de nuestra actuación, siempre nos aplaudían con mucho respeto.

–Unos papanatas con peluca empolvada, eso es lo que eran –intervino de nuevo el abuelo–. A mi me gustaban más las fiestas que se daban en las tabernas de los barrios pobres. Los jóvenes bebían y bailaban durante toda la noche y nunca perdían el compás.

–Abuela, si eramos tan felices con los humanos –exigió saber SI–, ¿por qué ahora estamos siempre huyendo de ellos?

–Tú eras muy pequeño entonces y por eso no te acuerdas –le explicó su madre–. Los humanos siguieron inventando máquinas cada vez más raras y, sobre todo, ruidosas.

–¿Nosotros? –me hice la despistada.

–Sí, unos artefactos cada vez más grandes y feos: unos vuelan, como los pájaros, otros corren más que los galgos, pero todos hacen mucho ruido.

– Ah, claro, te refieres a los aviones y a los coches –adiviné sin mucho esfuerzo–. Todo eso lo hemos inventado para hacer más cómoda nuestra vida.

–¿Cómo dices? ¿Unas máquinas que hacen un ruido infernal os hacen la vida más cómoda? –me echó en cara el abuelo DO, mientras el resto de la familia me miraba como si fuese el asesino más sanguinario de la historia.

–Sí... –balbuceé–, por ejemplo, los automóviles nos permiten llegar antes a los sitios y sin cansarnos.

–¿Te refieres a esos locos cacharros que no paran de chocar unos contra otros y matan a la gente que viaja dentro?

–Bueno, no siempre pasa eso –le contesté como pude a SI.

–Y no solo es el ruido –continuó la hermana de mi sonoro amigo–, echan un humo muy negro por un tubo y no te dejan respirar.

–Al principio había una o dos de esas máquinas con ruedas –completó la abuela con tristeza–, pero, luego, se convirtieron en millones y no pararon hasta atascar las calles y plazas de todas las ciudades.

–¡¡¡Oh!!!... –exclamaron a la vez SI y LA. Sin duda no esperaban el triste final de esta historia.

Todos los sonidos se quedaron en silencio y sus colores se fueron apagando, poco a poco. El azul intenso del abuelo DO, que se confundía con el radiante cielo del verano, se fue diluyendo en una gris tormenta de mar y el verde de la abuela RE, antes puro y vegetal, se transformó en una especie de mancha amarillenta de pus.

–Hijos míos, por eso abandonamos la ciudad, porque los seres humanos la han llenado de artefactos ensordecedores que están acabando con la música.

–¡Ajá! Os pillé.

El compositor pedante y cabezón saltó sobre nosotros y extendió sus gordos brazos para poder cogernos a todos. ¿De dónde había salido aquel monstruo presuntuoso y torpón? ¿Cómo pudo seguirme sin perderse, él que siempre confundía la puerta de salida con la del armario donde mi tía guardaba la escoba y el cubo de fregar el suelo? ¡Oh!... ahora me daba cuenta, yo tenía la culpa: no había tomado ninguna precaución para poder evitar que alguien me siguiera. Por mi culpa, PGA estaba apunto de atrapar a sus duendecillos de la música, como él mismo les llamaba.

Bueno, en teoría, el factor sorpresa le daba cierta ventaja, pero el fósforo andante se movía con tanta falta de coordinación que LA se le escapó por debajo de las piernas, su hermano SI saltó por encima de su espalda cuando se tropezó porque la abuela RE le había puesto la zancadilla, y SOL se libraba de sus manos dando un ligero movimiento de su pelvis, al más puro estilo de Elvis. Al final del baile, solo el abuelo DO se había dejado atrapar y ya se veía colgado en un cuadro en la pared al lado de una colección de mariposas.

–¡Déjele en paz! –le grité al músico de los supermercados a la vez que le daba una patada en el culo. Pero lo tenía tan grueso que ni se inmutó.

–¡Cállate ya, niña maleducada y sabelotodo! –me contestó PGA, mientras trataba de enrollar al abuelo con la cuerda que tiraba de la campana de la iglesia del pueblo.

–¡Eres un abusón! Atrápame a mí, si puedes.

–No me hace falta correr para atrapar a todos tus amiguitos. Ahora verás.

El músico sacó algo brillante de uno de sus bolsillos y, a duras penas, consiguió llevárselo a la boca. Estiró sus dedos regordetes y entonces pude ver cómo era aquel extraño objeto que relucía al sol. Se trataba de una flauta metálica. La había visto en esos conciertos de música clásica que suelen echar por la tele a las cinco de la madrugada. Pero, en vez de soplar, como hacían esos músicos, PGA se puso a sorber y chupar, con mucha fuerza, como si estuviera fumando un puro muy grande. Quizá así, al revés, tocaban los instrumentos en la lejana galaxia de donde procedía este extraterrestre.

Al abuelo DO también le sorprendió mucho esta maniobra, pero aprovechó la ocasión para deshacer la cuerda que oprimía sus piernas y, esta vez sí, salió corriendo a toda velocidad.

–Intenta atraparlo ahora, descerebrado con orejas –reté a PGA con una sonrisa de satisfacción.

La alegría de la victoria me duró bien poco. De la flauta de don Pelayo salió un pequeño tornado, que comenzó a tragarse todos los sonidos que había a su alrededor.

Tardé una milésima de segundo en descubrir lo que estaba ocurriendo. El extraterrestre había sacado su arma letal (una flauta aspiradora de sonidos) y los estaba capturando todos: desde el zumbido de las abejas al trino de los pájaros, pasando por el murmullo del agua de la fuente. La cosa se estaba poniendo realmente complicada y yo me puse a gritar, pero, por más que movía los labios, nada salía de mi boca.

Intenté hacer un último esfuerzo: grité "¡¡¡socorro!!!" con todas mis fuerzas, pero PGA volvió a succionar su flauta con más ganas y la abuela RE fue tragada antes de que pudiera pronunciar la primera "S".

Y el ente barrigón no se conformó con su primera víctima. Siguió succionando y succionando y atrapó también a la madre de SI, a su padre, que seguía durmiendo plácidamente como si nada estuviera pasando, y luego se tragó a SOL y a LA.

Solo faltaba SI, que se había refugiado en lo alto del campanario del pueblo abandonado. Podía ver perfectamente su cara de rabia, y por eso me abalancé sobre don Pelayo dispuesta a arrebatarle aquel instrumento diabólico, porque una niña de ciudad nunca abandona a sus colegas, aunque se hayan saltado tres semáforos en rojo. Sin embargo, la voz de SI me detuvo en seco.

–No te metas en esto –oí que me gritaba antes de que la flauta infernal se lo tragara por completo–. Solo nos quiere a nosotros. Tú tienes que escapar para poder rescatarnos.

PGA dejó de succionar y el tornado cesó. El pueblo abandonado parecía más abandonado que nunca. No se oía ni el viento, ni el agua de la fuente, ni los cantos de los pájaros... Es más, sin los sonidos, el aire parecía haberse congelado y empecé a marearme y casi me caigo redonda al suelo. Pero eso no fue lo peor: cuando me levanté, don Pelayo había desaparecido.

Ahora lo comprendía todo. Después de obtener su botín, el compositor extraterrestre seguro que había llamado a sus compañeros alienígenas y estos lo habían sacado de allí con un rayo de tele transportación que lanzaron desde su nave. Esto era tener mala suerte. PGA me había derrotado en mi propio terreno.

Esto no iba a quedar así. Debía rescatar a mis amigos, aunque estuvieran ya en los confines del Universo. Tenía que hacer tantos planes que decidí esa noche no bajar a cenar.

–Si no vienes pronto –me advirtió la pesada de mi tía por el hueco de la escalera–, le diré a tu madre que envíe por correo urgente el libro de matemáticas que, vaya casualidad, te dejaste olvidado en casa.

Bajé corriendo las escaleras. Mi plan de rescate podía esperar. Prefería ser atacada por un millón de marcianos cabreados antes que ponerme a hacer los deberes de mates. Seguro que las divisiones con decimales y las raíces cuadradas las habían inventado los policías. No hay ladrón que no confiese dónde está el dinero si le amenazan con ponerle un problema con raíces cuadradas.

–Ya voy, tía –me disculpé como pude.

–Uno, dos, tres...

Me senté de un salto en mi silla y... allí estaba. Inmóvil como una estatua griega de mármol. Enfrente de mí. Más tieso que una momia del museo egipcio. Indiferente. Con la mirada perdida. Más neutro que el champú que compra mi madre para que no chille cuando me lava el pelo. Y mis tíos seguían sonriendo y comiendo como si no hubiera pasado nada.

–Están muy buenos estos buñuelos de "bacalado", querida –le felicitó mi tío, que siempre se las daba de "fino" cuando tenía clientes sentados a su mesa.

–Los he hecho especialmente para ti, cariño.

Si supieran que estaban cenando con un secuestrador de familias inocentes, seguro que les daba un corte de digestión. Pero el compositor cabezota sabía disimular muy bien, con esa carita de inocente que ponen los asesinos en serie cuando les pilla la poli.

–Gracias, tesoro mío, no sabría qué hacer sin ti.

–De nada, amorcito.

Cuando se ponían en plan mimoso, mis tíos podían estar horas y horas mirándose el ombligo y sin enterarse de lo que estaba pasando a su alrededor. Es más, a esas horas, mis amigos podían estar encerrados en el más oscuro de los sótanos. No podía abrir la boca porque los adultos nunca creen lo que les cuentan los niños.

–Pilar, ¿llamo a tu madre por teléfono para pedirle ese libro al que tienes tanto cariño? –atacó de nuevo mi tía al darse cuenta de que ni siquiera había tocado mi cuchara.

–No, tía, por favor, que ya como, ya como...

Y una bombilla se encendió en mi cabeza. El cuchillo corta jamones de mi tío estaba detrás del salero, y con un ligero toque de muñeca...

–Discúlpenme, señores –dijo de repente el extraterrestre–. Creo que esta noche he comido demasiado y necesito dar un pequeño paseo para bajar la comida.

Eso de la telepatía (uno de los poderes de los seres de otros planetas) era un auténtico fastidio. Seguro que PGA había podido leer mi mente con la misma facilidad que una página de Internet.

–¡Tenga cuidado ahí fuera, don Pelayo! –le advirtió mi tío abriéndole el portón que daba al jardín–. Los lobos pueden andar cerca y, con el frío que está haciendo, creo que llevan bastantes meses sin llevarse nada decente a la boca.

El ente cabezón atravesó el jardín y yo me puse a comer como un elefante para tener la misma excusa y poder seguirle. Tal vez así podría descubrir dónde tenía encerrados a mis amigos, los sonidos de la escala musical.

—Vaya, lo que es capaz de hacer una mocosa para no estudiar matemáticas —concluyó mi tía al verme devorar su asquerosa sopa de fideos multicolores.

Pero el estómago me jugó una mala pasada. Acostumbrada a comer muy despacio, aquel atracón debió de atascar mi intestino grueso y acabé pasando el resto de la noche vomitando sobre la taza del retrete.

Justo comencé a recobrarme cuando salía el sol. La barriga todavía me daba vueltas, como el tambor de una lavadora, y por eso tardé un poco en encontrar la habitación de PGA. Estaba en el primer piso y era la única con calefacción, porque mis tíos odiaban pagar los recibos de la luz. Yo era de la familia y dormía en el desván, junto a las latas de conserva de los tiempos de los dinosaurios y en compañía de unas pieles de gato, que mi tío había puesto a secar para hacerse un abrigo. Él afirmaba que, con el cambio climático y la desaparición masiva de las especies salvajes, la caza de los felinos domésticos sustituiría a la de los bebés-foca.

Por fin, al séptimo intento, vi el camino despejado y me planté justo delante de la puerta del extraterrestre compositor. Abrí la cerradura con mucho sigilo y me acerqué de puntillas a la cabecera de su cama. El cuarto estaba muy oscuro y eso no facilitó la operación de ataque al estilo chino. Como no podía fallar de nuevo, palpé la cama para asegurarme de que había alcanzado la almohada, y deduje que la cabezota dormida de don Pelayo no andaría lejos. Levanté con las dos manos un viejo jarrón de porcelana que alguien había dejado en el desván y, con todas mis fuerzas, lancé el torpedo hacia mi objetivo. Pero este rebotó en la cama y, gracias a los muelles del colchón, se volvió hacia mí a mayor velocidad. Intenté agacharme para esquivarlo, pero la vomitona debió de estropear algunos circuitos en mi cerebro porque el jarrón chino impactó en mi esternón. ¡Vaya palabrota!, seguro que no la recordaría si mi profe de naturales no nos hubiera obligado a escribirla cien veces en nuestro cuaderno. Aquello me dolió un montón y, de nuevo, caí fulminada, esta vez, sobre la alfombra llena de pelos pegajosos de PGA. Mientras tanto, el maldito jarrón (tras rebotar en mi cuerpo) volvió a caer en la cama sin recibir el más mínimo rasguño.

–¡Pilar, Pilar!... –mi tío por fin logró despertarme después de echarme un cubo de agua helada.

–Sí... ¿qué pasa? –pregunté yo quitándome los cubitos de hielo de encima.

–Eso digo yo. ¿Qué haces en este cuarto?, ¿has venido a despedirte de don Pelayo?

–¿Regresa ya a la ciudad?

–Ya sabía yo que lo ibas a echar de menos. Eres como tu madre, por fuera pareces un bloque de acero, sin sentimientos, pero, por dentro, eres una sentimental y te encariñas con cualquiera, aunque no lo quieras reconocer.

–No puede irse, tío –protesté ansiosa. No podía permitir que me derrotara de nuevo ese barrigón de otro planeta–. Tenemos todavía un asuntillo pendiente.

–Ay, qué cariñosa eres... Bueno, en realidad, ya se ha ido esta mañana, muy temprano.

–¿No se lo comieron los lobos anoche? Yo oí ruidos muy raros en el jardín...

–Qué cosas tienes, Pilar –dijo mi tía que entraba con un juego de sábanas limpias–. No conozco a ningún lobo que se haya comido a un hombre, pero conozco a muchos hombres que han matado a un montón de lobos.

Don Pelayo se había fugado. ¿Dónde iba a encontrarlo si el mundo estaba lleno de tipos presumidos y fantasmas como él? En cada plaza, caminando por la acera o esperando el autobús podía encontrar docenas de bocazas pedantes prácticamente iguales. ¿Y si pegaba carteles dando una recompensa por su captura como hacían en las pelis del oeste? La idea no estaba mal, pero seguro que se presentarían muchos de candidatos a cabezón del año y, entonces, tendría que pagarles a todos y, como no tenía ni una maldita moneda, me perseguirían y acabaría en la cárcel, por no pagar mis deudas. Si fuera la dueña de un banco, todo sería distinto… los hombres se arrodillarían a mis pies para pedirme un préstamo y yo les inflaría a comisiones, gastos de apertura, cancelaciones anticipadas y certificados de tasación. ¡Cuánto dinero podría ganar en un solo día!... y hablando de dinero.

–Oye, tío –me acerqué dulcemente a él mientras arreglaba una parte de la cerca del jardín. Al principio lo hacía bien, con sus clavitos y todo, pero, cuando se daba tres martillazos seguidos en el dedo gordo, acababa dando patadas a todos los tablones de color verde chillón.

–¿Estás enferma, Pilar?

–No, no es eso. ¿Cuánto dinero te ha dejado a deber el extrate… digo, don Pelayo?

–No sé… –empezó a calcular rascándose la perilla. No tenía, pero eso le daba igual a mi tío. Siempre se la rascaba cuando se ponía a pensar en algo–. Creo que me debe tres comidas, dos cenas, tres noches y siete desayunos completos, ¿por qué?

–Por nada. ¡Vaya gorrón nos ha salido ese compositor cabezón!

–¡Pilar… no se habla así de las personas mayores! –me reprendió mi tío–, aunque, la verdad, gorrón sí que es, un maldito gorrón, diría yo, un imbécil gorrón, que se ha aprovechado de una pobre familia de campo y…

–Y… ¿no te gustaría cobrar?

–Claro, vaya pregunta. Ya he llamado a la policía, y no me han dado ninguna esperanza. Me han explicado que si no persiguen a los banqueros que cobran millones en comisiones, no entienden por qué tienen que ir detrás de un señor que solo debe un par de días de pensión completa.

–Si me dejaras salir en su busca… –intenté convencerle– lo atraparía esta misma noche.

–¿Estás loca, niña? Te puedes meter en un buen lío y tu madre me mataría.

–¿Cuánto dinero dices que te debe?

–Vale, ¿cuándo te vas?

En un acto de valentía, digno del héroe más valiente del mundo, mi tío se dispuso a entrar en la cocina sin hacer ruido. Los hombres tienen alergia a las cocinas. Es algo genético en ellos y por eso no se les ve nunca por allí. No obstante, esta vez, el hermano de mi madre tenía una buena razón para entrar. Traspasó la puerta, avanzó unos pasos de puntillas, abrió la nevera, introdujo la mano y… mi tía le mandó fregar los platos. Su padre había sido conserje en un colegio de pago y lo de pillar a la gente con las manos en la masa lo llevaba en la sangre.

Mi tío se tiró toda la mañana fregando los cacharros de la última comilona de don Pelayo, la olla grasienta del potaje semanal de alubias y los tenedores de toda la semana. Después mi tía le mandó limpiar los baldosines, y ese día descubrí que, en realidad, eran blancos y no negros como yo creía.

–Aquí tienes –mi tío me dio una bolsita con un par de trozos de pan seco y una salchicha petrificada–, es lo único que he podido sacar de la nevera sin que tu tía se diera cuenta.

–Gracias, tío, no te arrepentirás.

–No, si ya me estoy arrepintiendo, porque casi pierdo la vida ahí dentro, entre tanto cacharro sucio.

–No te preocupes: pronto atraparé a tu cliente gorrón y, con el dinero que te debe, podrás ir a comer al mejor restaurante de la ciudad y pedir un buen par de huevos fritos con…

–¡¡¡No, más platos no!!! –y se desmayó allí mismo.

Cogí mi mochila atrapa-pesados y, para aligerar peso, le di el salchichón a Ataulfo, el perro guardián de mi tío, un mastín viejo y con pulgas que más que ladrar a los extraños les lamía los pies en señal de sumisión. En fin, todo un depredador. A Ataulfo le encantaban las salchichas, pero, desde que se comió aquella, el veterinario dice que sufre diarrea crónica. Será por lo mal que le sienta el aire limpio del campo, digo yo.

Supongo que ahora os estaréis preguntando cómo una niña, como yo, y sin dinero, puede recorrer los 400 kilómetros largos que separan el campo de la ciudad. Pues muy sencillo: siempre hay algún conductor amable dispuesto a ayudarte.

Pero aquel sábado debía de ser el Día Internacional de los Conductores Bordes, porque ninguno quiso subirme cuando me puse a hacer autostop. Bueno, menos mal que se apiadó de mí el señor del camión amarillo que recogía los envases de plástico usados. Se tenía que parar cada 100 metros y todo iba bien... hasta que chocó contra una farola. No me extraña, como decía que era un trabajo muy monótono y aburrido, aparte de conducir, leía un cómic de superhéroes, confeccionaba la quiniela de la semana y chateaba con una chica brasileña por el móvil.

Los bomberos tuvieron que utilizar un abrelatas gigante para poder sacarnos entre los restos del metal de la farola y el chasis destrozado del camión. Me dolía un poco el pecho y no podía respirar. Entonces me di cuenta de que estaba en la ciudad. El olor nauseabundo de la depuradora, los tubos de escape de los autobuses y las chimeneas de la planta química, la térmica y la petrolífera, eran inconfundibles. Por fin había llegado a mi hogar.

Y todo estaba tal y como lo dejé. Las cacas de perro y los escupitajos en las aceras, la capa gris sobre mi cabeza, los socavones de las obras del metro... Hogar, dulce hogar. Recogí mis cosas del suelo, le di las gracias a un bombero con bigote y me dispuse a entrar, de nuevo, en mi territorio.

La gran ciudad es el hormiguero perfecto que han inventado los humanos. Existen multitud de galerías por donde meterse y por ellas pululan millones de personas, sin que nada ni nadie los detenga. Es un movimiento continuo: de allí para aquí, de acá para allá, los urbanitas están en todas partes y al mismo tiempo. Y son felices en su continuo deambular, aunque sus espaldas se acaben encorvando y sus ojos pierdan todo su brillo. Porque ¿para qué nos vamos a estirar para poder ver el cielo, si una capa de humo gris lo tapa todo?

Y por si fuera poco, en la gran ciudad lo tienes todo. Si tienes sed, siempre hay cerca alguna tubería de agua potable rota. Si tienes hambre, los cubos de la basura están abiertos todo el día. Algunos prefieren los locales de comida rápida, pero, al fin y al cabo, ¿no es lo mismo? Y si, después de comer, tienes un poco de sueño, qué mejor que un banco en el parque. Con música y todo, porque seguro que vendrán luego los de las litronas a cantarte un rato.

En una gran ciudad, nadie se siente solo. Las colas del metro te empujan a cualquier parte, las del cine te calientan en pleno invierno y en las de las comisarías puedes aprender el idioma más extraño del mundo.

Resumiendo, en la ciudad vivimos millones de personas y, supongo yo, que por algo será. Aunque ahora que lo pienso, con tanta gente moviéndose sin parar y pisándote los pies, ¡¿cómo voy a encontrar al compositor loco que robó los sonidos de la escala musical?!

Bueno, que no cunda el pánico. Lo primero que tengo que hacer es comprarme un buen callejero para no perderme y, después, claro está, la guía del ocio y toda la ciudad estará a mi entera disposición. ¡Ah!... se me olvidaba un pequeño detalle, más bien minúsculo, un problemilla, diría yo: de dónde iba a sacar el dinero. Lo más urgente, pues, era encontrar un ser ingenuo, desvalido, algo bobalicón... vamos, que se creyera cualquier cosa. Pero, ¿quedaban aún en nuestro planeta seres así?

–¡Hola, abuelo!

–Buenos días, Pilar, ¿qué haces levantada tan temprano un sábado, si aún no son las tres de la tarde?

–Bueno, abu, es que hoy no es un día cualquiera –mi abuelo era capaz de creerse la mentira más gorda del mundo, si se la contaba con algunas lagrimillas de más en los ojos. Y lo mejor de todo: acababa de cobrar su pensión.

–Vaya, vaya, ¿qué le pasa a mi nieta favorita? –me contestó vocalizando a duras penas. El mes pasado había tenido que vender su dentadura postiza para invitarme una tarde a ir al cine.

–Tú me ayudarás, ¿verdad, abu? –inmediatamente puse esa cara de perro faldero muriéndose de ganas de hacer pis, que tanto les impresiona a todos los abuelos de la Tierra.

–Claro que sí, Pilar, pero no me asustes.

–Estoy en peligro de muerte, abu.

–¡No me digas!, ¿te persigue la mafia?

–No, algo mucho peor: el gorila de mi colegio. Ese niño tiene cero gramos de masa cerebral, pero dinamita en sus músculos.

–¡No me digas!

–Sí, un día le pedí un poco de dinero para comprarme un bocadillo porque tenía mucha hambre. El profe de gimnasia nos obligó a dar siete vueltas al patio y había vomitado todo mi desayuno, así que…

–Y ahora tienes que devolverme el triple o, de lo contrario…

–Sí, abuelo.

–Y tú ni siquiera te planteas la segunda opción.

–No, abuelo. Soy aún muy joven para morir.

–Está bien, está bien –mi abuelo se lo había tragado todo. Era un poco gruñón, sobre todo en Navidad, cuando decía eso de "es mi última nochebuena y vengo a despedirme de todos", pero, en el fondo…–, ¿cuánto le debes? –concluyó.

–Para qué entrar en detalles sin importancia, abuelo, tú dime dónde escondes tu cartera y ya está.

Os aseguro que estaba dispuesta a dejarlo sin blanca, si el banco no lo hubiera hecho antes con sus comisiones. Solo había lo justo para comprar la guía del ocio y comer algo barato. Miré la página de los restaurantes y todos eran caros, carísimos, por las nubes, en otra galaxia… Así que no tuve más remedio que ir a la pizzería de la esquina y… estaba cerrada por vacaciones.

Desesperada, me refugié en un parque y pensé en el último remedio que me quedaba: taparme la nariz y engullir los trozos de pan seco que mi tío había conseguido jugándose la vida en la cocina. Tenía tanta hambre atrasada que abrí la mochila y los saqué con mucho cuidado. Inmediatamente me rodeó un ejército de palomas raquíticas. Las miré, asustada, y ellas a mí. Estaban dispuestas a sacarme los ojos a picotazos si no les daba hasta la última miga. Yo quise correr, pero las más gordas me cortaron el paso mientras las más jóvenes me picoteaban el pelo con sus vuelos en rasante. Abrí la boca para pedir ayuda y casi me trago entero un pichón que había calculado mal su plan de vuelo. Aquel enjambre de bichos con alas me tenían completamente cercada y la fuerza de gravedad hizo el resto. Tropecé, los dos trozos de pan se me escaparon de las manos y fueron devorados antes de que pudieran tocar el suelo.

No me dejaron ni una migaja. Tan de repente como llegaron, se fueron y, sin obstáculos tapándome la visión, pude ver la primera cola de gente. El hambre mejora la vista y no la zanahoria, como dice mi madre, porque, en la otra esquina divisé otra cola, y al final de la calle, una tercera, y la cuarta, más allá y la quinta, la sexta, la séptima, la octava… ya no me sabía más números cardinales, pero todavía quedaban más colas.

Las rebajas habían terminado hacía un mes, así que no entendía por qué la gente se arremolinaba frente a un supermercado, una tienda de ropa de diseño, una zapatería, dos joyerías y… ¡una funeraria!

¿Todo el mundo se había vuelto loco? O cambio la pregunta: ¿todo el mundo se había vuelto doblemente loco? Aquello no tenía explicación. Mi mente me pedía a gritos: "!Sal corriendo de aquí y no pares... hasta esconderte detrás de tu abuelo!".

Mi abuelo todavía guardaba en el desván un viejo fusil de cuando le engañaron para ir a la guerra. Lo malo es que también engañaron a los del pueblo de al lado y estuvieron tres años pegándose tiros unos a otros, y eso que no tenían ningún motivo para pelear. Hacía años que mi abuela había usado la pólvora de los cartuchos para condimentar las lentejas, pero me daba igual. Un abuelo con fusil es un buen repelente para que los niños más grandes que tú no te peguen durante el recreo.

Mi mente no paraba de hablar y hablar y se estaba poniendo pesadísima, como de costumbre. Que si esto, que si lo otro, que si además, que mira tú por dónde. Me tapé las orejas y decidí hacerle caso a mi estómago, como siempre. De la primera cola salía un tufillo a hamburguesa con salsa picante y eso es algo que un niño de ciudad es incapaz de rechazar.

Primero intenté colarme, pero algunos empezaron a silbar y, una vez descubierta, me dedicaron todo tipo de piropos. Acepté mi derrota (sin duda mi estancia en el campo había debilitado mi inteligencia urbanita) y me acerqué a un señor con bigote que cerraba la fila.

–Eh, niña, no intentes colarte, que tienes cara de listilla.

–Oiga, ¿por qué hay tanta gente haciendo cola? –le pregunté para despistar.

–¿No te has enterado? –y... ¡¡milagro!!, aquel señor tan serio comenzó a tatarear una cancioncilla–: "Coge una hamburguesa, coge dos... no seas tonto, si puedes comer cuatro, también 32".

Ahora estaba segura. Por la mañana, al abrir la nevera para prepararme el desayuno, mi tía debió de confundir la botella de leche con el ron, que guardaban para las mejores visitas. ¡Un triste oficinista, un burócrata del papel, un sacerdote de los formularios oficiales, un guardián de los secretos de la administración estaba cantando una cancioncilla al más puro estilo de los cantantes de quinceañeras! Algo no encajaba. Algo no funcionaba. Algo olía… a pescado podrido.

El hombre del traje oscuro me señaló dos altavoces que habían colgado a la entrada de la Hamburguesería. Estaban llenos de grasa, pero, por primera vez, oí en la calle una de esas melodías pegadizas de las que me había hablado el compositor lunático que se había alojado en la casa rural de mis tíos. La melodía era sencilla. Sin adornos. Con unas pocas notas musicales, repartidas por aquí y por allá, pero era tan fresca y pegadiza, que se te metía en el cerebro y, a los pocos segundos, ya estabas llevando el compás y canturreando la letra: "Coge una hamburguesa, coge dos… no seas tonto, si puedes comer cuatro, también 32".

Y, claro, de tanto cantarla, te entraban unas ganas locas de comer hamburguesas y la cola llegaba ya a la otra esquina. Y lo mismo ocurría en todos los supermercados, tiendas de todo tipo y locales de comida que pude ver.

–Antes, cuando salían los anuncios en la tele, me iba a hacer pis –le confesaba una señora muy "fashion" a otra–. Ahora, hago al revés: cuando echan la película, me levanto enseguida del sofá. ¡Menudo aburrimiento, no tener nada que comprar!

–Ah, sí, chica, ¡qué emocionante es ver esas casas llenas de objetos de diseño y que están a muy buen precio!

–Mi marido prefiere los anuncios de coches… y yo, los de cremas y demás potingues antiarrugas. Si no las compro todas, no puedo reafirmar mi personalidad. El otro día, sin ir más lejos, salí a la calle sin untarme el cutis y volví corriendo… ¡me sentía completamente desnuda!

–Chica, sí, ¡qué fastidio! Con tantos tonos de lápiz de labios que salen en la tele, una ya no sabe cuál elegir. Yo me los llevo todos y así no me frustro.

–Quita, quita, nuestras madres ahorraban demasiado. Las cosas han cambiado afortunadamente: estar siempre joven requiere muchos cuidados.

La música seguía sonando en plena calle y la gente entraba en manada en tiendas y supermercados. Cuando alguno de los establecimientos tenía que cerrar por haber agotado sus existencias, abucheaban a los pobres dependientes.Y cuando otro volvía a abrir, la gente rompía a aplaudir y entraba a empujones arrollando todo lo que encontraban a su paso, cochecitos de bebé incluidos.

Quise huir de allí, pero mis piernas no me respondían. Sin que me diera cuenta, la música había invadido mi mente y mis pies dejaron de obedecerme.Yo les ordené que salieran corriendo, pero mis zapatillas de deporte se dirigieron a la cola que estaba más cerca.

De repente, me vi dentro de un huracán de cuerpos, que se pegaban por entrar en una tienducha pequeña y oscura. Creo que era de pijamas y, por los modelos expuestos en el escaparate minúsculo, uno se percataba de que no habían vendido ninguno desde hacía años.

Sin embargo, ahora, los clientes los arrancaban de los maniquís con las mismas ganas que un niño se come un helado en pleno agosto. ¿Cómo se había producido este milagro? Los de atrás me empujaron un poco más y, entonces, pude escucharlo: aquel antro pijamil tenía su propio anuncio musical, con letra y todo:

–"Entra aquí, entra aquí" –cantaban varias voces de mujer, las más hermosas que había oído nunca–. "Tenemos pijamas, medias y calcetines. Compra todo y tendrás… unos días de oro".

Reuniendo todas mis fuerzas, quise frenar en seco, pero la canción era tan pegadiza que mi cuerpo solo deseaba ya una cosa: entrar en la tienda y comprarme una tonelada de pijamas, aunque no me hicieran ninguna falta.

Solo había una solución: me tapé los oídos y me puse a pensar en otra cosa. Mi libro de inglés, un paisaje submarino, una puerta de madera, un pijama, un pijama con lunares rosas, un pijama corto de terciopelo, un pijama de cintas de seda, un pijama...

Mis piernas andaban sin control y tropecé contra el cristal de la puerta del establecimiento. Del tortazo, mi nariz comenzó a sangrar y, para limpiarme, cogí un papel que estaba pegado. ¿Un papel? No, aquello era una foto, una foto de alguien que me era familiar. Sí, yo había visto antes esa calva reluciente. Empecé a fijarme más y comprobé que debajo de la imagen había también estas letras:

"EXPECTACIÓN EN EL MUNDO DE LA PUBLICIDAD. El insigne compositor universal Pelayo García Ansuátegui mostrará su "Máquina Musical de Los Deseos", diseñada por su genial mente, a los más importantes publicistas del mundo en la Reunión Extraordinaria que hoy se celebrará en nuestra ciudad".

Y allí estaba él en la fotografía: sonriendo como una morsa miope y exhibiendo una máquina llena de botones. Así que ahora se había convertido en un "Músico Universal" y había cambiado su bermuda de color chillón y la camiseta con frutas tropicales por un traje negro de pingüino.

–¿Cuántos pijamas quieres, niña? –la vocecilla de ratón de un dependiente me devolvió a la cruda realidad–. Decídete pronto... que me taponas la cola y hay mucha peña esperando su turno.

–Perdona... tengo que salir de aquí –me disculpé como pude–, tengo una cita con este tipo de la foto.

–¿Con don Pelayo? –me miró supersorprendido.

–Sí, ¿sabes quién es?

–Vaya bromista que estás hecha, ¿quién no conoce al músico más famoso del mundo, al autor de las canciones de anuncios más famosas del mundo, al compositor de las canciones que están ganando todos los festivales del mundo, al...

–Para, para... ya veo que te sabes toda su vida.

–Por supuesto, gracias al anuncio que nos compuso él en un pispás, no me han echado a la calle y ahora el negocio funciona superguay y me van a ascender a dependiente de Tercera y... –cayó de pronto en la cuenta–, ¿Y tú quién demonios eres, si puede saberse?

–Soy su sobrina –me escaqueé–, su sobrina... del campo.

–¡Eh, jefe!, ¡¡jefe!... –el dependiente se puso a aullar como la sirena de una ambulancia–, esta niña es familiar de don Pelayo, el famoso compositor.

–¡Qué honor para nosotros!, ¡qué honor tan grande! –el dueño de la tienda de pijamas se abrió paso entre el mogollón de gente, empujando sin ningún miramiento a todo el que se cruzaba en su camino.

–¿Ha estado aquí ese... ese?... –empecé a balbucear.

–¿Ese benefactor del comercio mundial? –me corrigió con extrema amabilidad–. Sí, niña mía, acaba de irse hace apenas unos segundos. ¿No lo percibes?, todavía puede olerse su magnánima fragancia en todo mi local. Hasta ayer, en "Pijamas Manolín" no éramos capaces de vender ni un mísero hilo, pero hoy, con la inestimable ayuda de tu tío, nos arrancan el género hasta del escaparate, que está lleno de cucarachas y moho de no usarse.

–Ya veo, ya...

–La gente entra y, sin mirar el precio, compra y compra todo lo que pilla. Hasta acabamos de vender los últimos calcetines para bebé, amarillo limón, que llevaban aquí desde que mi tatarabuelo abrió esta tienda. Creo que está de moda usarlos como funda para el teléfono móvil.

Y me contó su historia. Don Pelayo llegó con su máquina y dio un par de vueltas a la tienda. Después miró el techo, pulsó unos botones y... esperó. Al poco tiempo, la máquina escupió un disco muy finito y le dijo al dueño del establecimiento que lo pusiera a todo volumen en el equipo de sonido, para que la gente pudiera oírlo desde la calle. El resto ya lo conocen: clientes de todo tipo y condición llenaron la tienda de pijamas y medias.

–Por cierto, tengo unas medias estupendas para ti, niña –me propuso el dueño dando por finalizada su historia–. Están llenas de agujeros por un fallo de fabricación, pero... me las quitan de las manos, porque un anuncio ha puesto de moda las medias agujereadas, como los quesos "gruyère".

–Gracias por la oferta –traté de escaquearme–, me tengo que ir, mi tío me está esperando.

–No olvides darle recuerdos de nuestra parte y dile que, por supuesto, le seguiré mandando su comisión por el extraordinario crecimiento de las ventas.

–¿Y no podía darme a mí un pequeño adelanto?

Me metió tantas monedas y billetes en los bolsillos que casi no pude salir de la tienda de lo pesada que me sentía. ¡Bahhh!... la alegría por el dinero fácil tampoco me duró mucho. La reunión de don Pelayo con los mejores publicistas del mundo se iba a celebrar en un edificio de diseño situado en pleno centro, y tuve que untar a dos porteros, cinco guardias jurados y tres guardaespaldas con pistola, para que me dejaran entrar.

Además, por un pellizco más de billetes, conseguí que un conserje me indicara la sala exacta donde iba a celebrarse tan especial evento. Por suerte, la reunión todavía no había comenzado y pude colarme sin levantar sospechas.

No había nadie, pero la máquina ya estaba allí. Era un armatoste supersofistacado: miles de cables extrafinos salían de un agujerito y se colaban por otro. Había botones por todas partes (me recordaban a mis granos cuando tuve la varicela) y despedían luces multicolores. Me acerqué e intenté ponerla en marcha (de algo tenían que servir las clases de informática que nos dan desde la guardería), pero me deprimí al averiguar que solo se encendía al reconocer tu huella digital.

Me cabreé bastante, le dí un empujón y… unas horribles sirenas arrancaron como si tratara de robar el Banco de Londres. Me quedé petrificada. A las paredes les salieron unos pinchos muy gordos y una serpiente gigantesca se despertó a pocos metros de donde yo estaba.

–¡Eh, solo soy una niña! –grité al darme cuenta de que me había metido de golpe en la peor de mis pesadillas–. No pensaba tocar nada, solo estoy de visita.

Una trampilla se abrió bajo mis pies y… caí en un profundo agujero justo cuando la serpiente se disponía a darme un buen bocado. A partir de ahí, mis recuerdos se desvanecen entre la niebla.

Alguien me dio un tortazo y abrí los ojos, con unas ganas tremendas de devolverle el favor. ¡No hay derecho! Al final tuve que conformarme con darle una patada al aire porque allí no había nadie más que yo.

Los ojos se me llenaron de lágrimas de cocodrilo, pero pude ver que estaba acostada en una cama recién hecha y llena de ositos de peluche. Unos eran blancos y vestían como Santa Claus.

Otros eran bomberos o pilotos de aviones de combate, y el más grande llevaba la chaqueta azul de los policías. Sin duda estaba en la habitación del niño más mimado del mundo, es decir, don Pelayo. Y pronto conseguí la prueba definitiva: junto a la cama, habían colocado un piano completamente blanco, tanto... que las teclas brillaban igual que los dientes de un hipopótamo sin caries.

Ante esta visión, mi primer impulso fue ponerme a chillar: ¡¡¡SOCORRO!!! , como cuando mi madre me encerró por primera vez en una guardería y destrocé los tímpanos de las cuidadoras. Sin embargo, esta vez, algo en mi cerebro me hizo dar marcha atrás. Me incorporé muy despacio y me puse a reflexionar.

"¡¡¡SOCORRO!!!" –me puse a berrear presa del pánico–.

Pero, ¿quién me iba a oír si aquella habitación no tenía ni puertas ni ventanas? Pensé en provocar un incendio, pero la idea de morir achicharrada tampoco parecía muy divertida que digamos. Así que, a falta de otra diversión, me puse a aporrear el teclado con los pies. Al fin y al cabo, desde pequeña, siempre me había gustado el arte. Y en esa tarea creativa estaba concentrada, cuando se abrió el techo y descendió flotando una especie de guardián, con porra de rayos láser.

–¡Salvaje, deja el piano en paz, que me estás perforando las orejas!

–No, gracias, estoy componiendo una pieza de música contemporánea.

–¡¡Niña... detente, por favor, que me vas a dejar sordo... para toda la vida!!

–No, hasta que me reciba don Pelayo.

–¿Estás loca, enana del demonio? –me contestó con guasa.

–Pues sigo con mi sinfonía moderna para piano y... zapatilla de deporte.

–Lo que pides es imposible: en estos momentos, don Pelayo está reunido con los mejores publicistas del mundo y... no se le puede molestar.

Ayayah... me temía lo peor. Tenía que escapar de allí lo antes posible, para chafarle el plan de invadir musicalmente todo el planeta Tierra. Necesitaba encontrar una solución, y rápido. Estrujé mis neuronas igual que mi madre cuando me hace un zumo de naranja para desayunar y...

–¡El piano está desafinado!

–¿Estás segura, niña? –se alarmó el guardia de seguridad–. Es el piano favorito de don Pelayo.

–Pues está fatal, fatal –me hice la experta–. ¿No lo oye?

–¡Está bien, está bien! –aceptó angustiado el vigilante, metiéndose debajo de la cama para escapar del terremoto sonoro que estaba yo provocando–. Voy a llamar a mis compañeros para sacar el piano de aquí, pero tú me tienes que prometer que te meterás en la cama y que estarás quietecita. ¿Vale?

–Sí, prometido –le contesté dejando de tocar.

–Si algo malo le pasa al piano, don Pelayo nos ha amenazado con tirarnos a una piscina llena de caimanes.

El guardia de seguridad salió de su escondite y se puso a hablar con el exterior, utilizando una pulsera plateada que llevaba en la muñeca. ¿Veis como yo tenía razón: que son todos extraterrestres y que PGA es su cabecilla?

–¡Código Rojo! ¡Código Rojo! –ordenó–. Hay que sacar el piano de la habitación antes de que don Pelayo se de cuenta de que está desafinado.

Yo di un salto para meterme en la cama, pero fue una simple maniobra de distracción. El osito de peluche grande acabó tapado por las sábanas y yo debajo del piano.

Se oyó un pitido profundo, la pared del fondo se desvaneció y entró otro grupo de seres de otra galaxia. Un alienígena con gafas verdes y mono rosa tapó el piano con una manta ignífuga (¡Vaya palabrota!, ¿verdad? Nunca pensé que usaría palabras así, pero estaba escrito en la etiqueta de la tela y una se aburre cuando se esconde) y esto facilitó mi huída. El piano comenzó a moverse y, con un par de saltitos, pude escapar sin levantar ningún tipo de sospecha.

–Niña, duérmete un rato, que esto va para largo –oí que me decía el primer vigilante, mientras la pared regresaba a su sitio tras accionar un punto de luz.

Pronto se cansaron de arrastrar el instrumento y lo dejaron en mitad de un pasillo oscuro. Tapada por la manta, el aire se hacía irrespirable y, aunque era un escondite seguro, no tuve más remedio que abandonarlo. Busqué el cuarto de baño por una necesidad personal (que no pienso detallar) y, después de abrir varias puertas, me topé con la Sala de Juntas.

Pensé en pedir ayuda a la policía, pero... ¿qué les iba a contar?, ¿que un comando de extraterrestres había secuestrado una niña para exhibirla en un circo de su planeta? "Pasen y vean, pasen y vean, una niña terrícola, seguro que nunca han visto algo más horrible", dirían por los altavoces.

La verdad, no sabía qué camino tomar... hasta que volví a oír la chirriante voz de PGA:

–Señores míos y señoras mías, estimados jerifaltes del mundo de la Publicidad, son ustedes héroes, porque son capaces de vender cualquier cosa (por insignificante que sea) a cualquier cliente, por tonto que sea. Pongo por caso: un peine para calvos, cremas antiarrugas para mujeres de más de 80 o coches de carrera para conductores que viven en calles atascadas.

Un tímido aplauso interrumpió su discurso. Se notaba a la legua que todos eran jefes: aplaudían sin ningún tipo de fervor, porque estaban completamente convencidos de que las grandes ideas solo se les ocurren a los de su clase.

–Gracias, gracias –retomó de nuevo su discurso don Pelayo–. Yo les anuncio que ha llegado una nueva Era. A partir de ahora ya no serán individuos aislados los que compren objetos inútiles. No. Gracias a la máquina que tengo delante, la gente comprará todo lo que salga al mercado. Y su deseo será tan irresistible, que lo comprarán sea lo que sea y, sobre todo, valga lo que valga.

–¿Y cómo lo va a lograr, si puede saberse? –le interrumpió un hombre trajeado y con peluquín de diseño.

–¡Con mi música! –le desafió don Pelayo mirándole a los ojos. Seguro que así podía lanzarle mejor sus rayos paralizantes invisibles–. Es más. Con esta máquina que he diseñado, soy capaz de componer, en cuestión de segundos, la música más pegadiza y arrebatadora que jamás hayan oído. Sin darse cuenta, sus notas atraparán su mente y ya nunca podrán dejar de oírla. Y si a mi música le añadimos un ligero mensaje publicitario, el milagro se completa. Cualquiera que la oiga querrá comprar lo que yo quiera que compre. ¿Está claro?

Don Pelayo abrió un enorme ventanal de par en par y decenas de sus melodías invadieron la sala de juntas con sus estribillos pegadizos.

–Acérquense y oigan, ¡¡¡éste es MI MILAGRO!!!: la música arrastra a las masas hasta los centros comerciales, con la misma eficacia que el flautista de Hamelín capturaba a las ratas.

¿De qué me suena a mí el tipo ese? Y en ello estaba cuando los Jefes de Publicidad más importantes del mundo se agolparon junto a la ventana y empezaron a exclamar:

–¡Fantástico! ¡¡Extraordinario!! ¡¡¡Es el negocio del Siglo!!!

–No, disculpen, es el negocio del... Milenio –les corrigió el compositor extraterrestre, mostrando sus dientes de morsa–. No se me cansen demasiado, que todavía tenemos que hablar del dinero que cuesta acceder a los servicios de mi máquina. Hagamos un pequeño paréntesis. En la sala de al lado tienen un cóctel de comida de autor. Pasen y beban, que cuando estén más contentos, podremos hablar del precio más cómodamente.

Con las gráficas de las ganancias iluminando sus ojos, los Reyes de la Publicidad fueron abandonando la sala con la intención de llenar también sus estómagos.

–Por fin, ¡¡¡EL MUNDO ES MÍO!!! –se le escapó a don Pelayo nada más verse solo.

–Ejem, ejem... un momento –le corté yo la inspiración–, ¿no le parece que está exagerando un poco?

El culo prominente de PGA dio media vuelta y pude ver la mueca de rabia que aprisionaba sus regordetes labios. Más que un rostro aquella cara parecía una máscara de carnaval del conde Drácula.

–¡¿Quién osa en desafiarme?! –bramó como una mula atacada por un enjambre de moscas.

Como soy tan pequeña, defecto de familia, al principio no acertaba a verme. La Sala de Juntas era espaciosa y eso tampoco ayudaba mucho, que digamos, pero la situación mejoró bastante cuando se puso sus gafas de miope.

–¡Ah, eres tú, niña insolente, maleducada, mentirosilla, roñosa, comecaca, debilucha...

Etc., etc., etc. El ente calvorota habría estado todo el día dedicándome los más delicados piropos, si no hubiera aprovechado la ocasión para subirme a la mesa de Juntas, correr hacia la máquina, atraparla y abalanzarme contra el ventanal, que continuaba aún abierto de par en par. Levanté los brazos y...

–¡Niña simpática, no tires por la ventana mi Máquina Musical de los Deseos, que la vas a pulverizar!

–Vaya sorpresa, no sabía que era también adivino, porque eso es exactamente lo que voy a hacer.

–¡¡Noooo!! –se deprimió el compositor pedante–. Esa máquina vale miles de millones.

–Y a mí qué. Yo soy una niña pequeña y mis padres no me dejan tener dinero.

–Mira, reflexiona –hizo un último esfuerzo supremo para negociar conmigo–. Si te bajas de la mesa y me la devuelves sin ningún desperfecto, te daré... te daré... un caramelo.

Así de tacaño era don Pelayo. Ni siquiera en el momento más crítico de su vida, cuando veía esfumarse su sueño de ser el habitante más rico de la Galaxia, era capaz de rascarse un poco el bolsillo.

–Está bien, está bien. Te daré... dos caramelos. Uno para cada mano.

–Don Pelayo –le comuniqué solemnemente estirando del todo mis brazos. La máquina pesaba lo suyo y estaba deseando deshacerme del aparato–, despídase de su invento... para siempre.

–Tres caramelos y una gominola.

¡Habráse visto tanta generosidad! Aquello acabó de cabrearme. Tomé impulso con la cadera y...

–¡No nos mates, por favor!

La voz de SI resonó en mis oídos con la nitidez del primer día. No me lo podía creer. Dicen en la tele que, durante las situaciones límite, la mente humana te suele jugar malas pasadas.

–Cuatro caramelos de menta y dos gominolas de fresa.

Ahora o nunca, pensé. Jamás tendría otra oportunidad tan buena para destruir esta máquina maligna. Y no solo lo hacía por mí. La vida de mucha gente dependía de mi determinación. La vida de esos ciudadanos pacíficos a los que don Pelayo había transformado en robots dispuestos a comprar cualquier cosa.

–¡No tires la máquina por la ventana! –oí de nuevo la voz de SI–, toda mi familia está aquí dentro.

–Cinco caramelos y tres gominolas.

–¡Acepto!

Don Pelayo había vuelto a ganar. Bajé los brazos y deposité la máquina sobre la mesa de la Sala de Juntas. Inmediatamente me vi rodeada por un escuadrón de guardias con muy malas pintas. Sus uniformes olían a tabaco barato.

–¡Enciérrenla en el cuarto de los ratones! –ordenó el compositor con evidente satisfacción.

En el fondo, don Pelayo seguía siendo un niño... con pantalones largos.

–Y también llévense esta máquina de aquí –completó sus instrucciones–. Deposítenla en la caja fuerte, no quiero que ningún mocoso la vuelva a tocar nunca más con sus sucias manos.

PGA abandonó la habitación dando saltitos de rana, y los guardias debían de tener las orejas de madera porque lo liaron todo. Dejaron la máquina en el cuarto de los ratones y, en cambio, a mí intentaron meterme en la caja fuerte. Menos mal que me di cuenta de su intención y estiré mi cuello todo lo que pude. Al percatarse de que mi cuerpo no cabía, decidieron llevarme también al cuarto de los ratones de la Mansión del compositor. En resumen, gracias a su ineptitud, la máquina diabólica y yo nos juntábamos de nuevo.

Allí todo estaba oscuro, pero tenía tantas ganas de volver a ver a mis amigos del campo que reprimí mi pánico. Lo mismo me pasa con los ascensores: tengo claustrofobia cuando tengo que bajar, pero si hay que subir siete pisos, se me pasa enseguida y entro, como si nada. Qué curioso, ¿no?

–Eh, amigos. ¿Estáis todos bien? –pregunté acercando mis labios a una de las paredes metálicas de la máquina y... casi me electrocuto.

–¡Cuidado, pequeña! –me advirtió desde el interior la abuela RE–. Esto está lleno de trampas.

–¿Qué hacéis ahí dentro toda la familia, si puede saberse? –contraataqué yo. La curiosidad infantil no tiene límites.

–¿Qué te parece? –entró en juego el abuelo DO–. Estamos de vacaciones.

Se me ocurrían mil lugares distintos donde me gustaría pasar mis vacatas, pero lo de meterme en una caja de zapatos, de momento, no entraba en mis planes, al menos, los más próximos.

–Abuelo, cállate, que lo vas a estropear todo.

–Hola, LA –saludé con educación a la hermana de SI–. ¿Os estáis divirtiendo ahí dentro?

–¿Estás de broma o qué? –el abuelo DO volvía a enfadarse–. Mira que son tontos estos niños humanos. ¡Nos ha encerrado aquí ese músico energúmeno y nos hace trabajar a destajo todos los días!

–Sí, pequeña –por primera vez la abuela RE estaba de acuerdo con su marido–. Nosotros somos los que componemos esas melodías tan pegadizas. Don Pelayo nos obliga. Si no lo hacemos, nos amenaza con destruirnos con una pistola de rayos láser.

–Y nuestros anuncios musicales son todo un éxito –completó el más vanidoso de los sonidos–.

–Calla, abuelo –le cortó su hija, la dulce FA–, lo que estamos haciendo no es nada bueno: la música y la letra de nuestros spots publicitarios es tan irresistible que la gente sale a la calle y, sin poder contenerse, arrasa los centros comerciales.

–Es una especie de encantamiento musical, pero negativo –concluyó la abuela RE.

–¿Y si os negáis a crear esa música, a partir de ahora? –preguntó la ingenua de mí.

–Ya te lo hemos dicho –aclaró SI–. Ese músico lunático nos ha amenazado con liquidarnos a todos y nosotros somos simples sonidos, no podemos enfrentarnos a él. Además, nos ha encerrado aquí, en esta cárcel para sonidos y no podemos salir.

–¡Por favor, tienes que sacarnos de aquí! –insistió toda la familia al unísono.

–Por supuesto, soy una niña con muchos recursos.

Quizá exageré un poco. Me pasé todo el día intentando abrir aquella máquina, pero todo… todo… fue inútil. Aquel artilugio electrónico no tenía ningún agujero, sus paredes eran viscosas y sus botones te daban una descarga eléctrica cada vez que acercaba uno de mis dedos.

—Ya os lo dije yo —se resignó con sorna el abuelo DO—. Ningún humano sirve para nada.

—¿Has intentado desbloquear la puerta de entrada con tu huella dactilar? —me propuso SI.

—Sí, pero tampoco funciona.

Aquello no era una máquina, sino un ataúd electrónico, un sarcófago lleno de cables… en fin, una cámara acorazada diseñada por los extraterrestres.

Solo me quedaba un recurso: la popular patada, y en ello estaba cuando oímos unos pesados pasos que se acercaban por el pasillo.

—Escóndete, rápido —me aconsejó SI sin dudarlo—. Viene el guardia.

—¿Cómo sabes que es él?

—Por el ruido que hacen sus pies, es él… o un elefante cojo, tú eliges.

—Muy gracioso.

En las situaciones límite, sé por experiencia que te pueden pasar dos cosas: que te mueras de miedo o que, por primera vez, tus neuronas se pongan a trabajar en serio. Por suerte, a mí me pasó lo segundo. Mis circuitos cerebrales se tostaron como una pizza y, de pronto, lo tuve todo claro. Tenía la solución en la punta de la lengua.

—¡Atención, familia! —les comuniqué rebosante de alegría—. Ya sé cómo sacaros de ahí.

—¿Dándole un par de martillazos a la máquina?

—Abuelo, cierra la boca de una vez, y no digas más tonterías —le lanzó un ultimátum su mujer. ¿No ves que los ojos de la niña lanzan chispas? Eso es una magnífica señal.

En un pispás pusimos en marcha mi plan. Sabíamos que el vigilante vendría pronto a por la Máquina, así que solo tuve que esperar. Cuando el energúmeno abrió los pesados cerrojos de la puerta, me puse a patalear y chillar como una imbécil, una de mis especialidades, a la que suelo recurrir cuando mis padres no me compran la ropa que me gusta.

–¡Tengo pis, tengo pis!

–¿Y no te puedes aguantar, ni un poquito? –me pidió el guardia usando el característico mal humor de los "con porra"–. Don Pelayo me ha ordenado que le lleve su máquina inmediatamente a la Sala de Juntas y no sabes cómo se enfada cuando no se cumplen sus órdenes.

–Es que no me puedo aguantar más.

–Vaya caprichito, nena.

–¿Quiere que me mee aquí o… me deja ir sola al servicio?

–Venga, venga –accedió por fin–. Ve y vuelve corriendo al cuarto de los ratones. Los invitados están a punto de regresar de comer y don Pelayo nos ha dicho que no quiere verte husmeando por aquí.

¡Menudo palacio se había comprado el compositor pedante! El suelo era de mármol, las paredes tenían incrustaciones de marfil y los grifos goteaban agua plateada. El papel higiénico olía a grosellas del bosque y la bañera relucía como la sopera de porcelana que mi mamá solo saca para celebrar la Navidad. Había tantas cosas hermosas a mi alrededor que casi me olvido de escapar.

–Venga niña, que la reunión de los publicistas va a comenzar y tengo que encerrarte otra vez en el cuarto oscuro.

Aquel vigilante era un auténtico tostón.

–Es que también tengo caca y, al estar tanto tiempo encerrada, se me ha hecho un tapón en el culo y…

–Vale, vale, no hace falta que entres en detalles.

Me quedaba muy poco tiempo. Levanté la vista para comprobar si el techo también era de mármol y… allí estaba: el conducto del aire acondicionado. Me subí al lavabo y abrí la rejilla de la ventilación. El tubo era bastante estrecho, pero no tenía elección si quería escapar. Me metí a presión y, al poco rato, ya estaba andando a gatas por esa especie de pasadizo. El aire frío me golpeaba la nariz y muy pronto me hice un lío. El tubo giraba a la derecha, luego otras dos veces a la izquierda, para después subir y subir y...vuelta a empezar.

"¡Socorro!", –grité al darme cuenta de que me había perdido en este laberinto de tubos congelados. Nadie me oyó. Estaba atrapada y me pudriría antes de que a mis padres se les ocurriera buscarme aquí.

Estaba perdida, me dolían todos los huesos (desde el pulgar del pie derecho al maxilar superior) y ya empezaba a resignarme a morir allí dentro cuando volví a oír la vocecilla desagradable de don Pelayo.

–Amigos publicista de todo el mundo, ¿estamos todos de acuerdo en realizar la primera campaña mundial utilizando mi máquina mágica?

El "sí" retumbó en todo el tubo metálico del aire acondicionado, y casi se desploma el techo.

–Gracias a mi máquina, todas las tiendas del mundo tendrán su propio anuncio con la música más pegadiza e irresistible que hayan oído nunca.

–¡Fenomenal!, ¡¡fantástico!!, ¡¡¡viva don Pelayo, el músico universal!!!

Los vítores sonaban tan fuertes que el tubo del aire acondicionado volvió a ponerse a temblar, y yo imaginaba que estaba cabalgando a lomos de un caballo salvaje.

–Aquí les dejo la máquina –explicó PGA a su entregado público–. Solo tienen que teclear una frase, un lema para un anuncio publicitario y la máquina le añadirá una melodía tan cautivadora que enseguida se agotarán todas las existencias mundiales del producto que quieran promocionar.

Los aplausos no me dejaron escuchar más. Con tantas vibraciones, ahora sí que tenía unas ganas locas de hacer pis, pero tuve que esperar hasta que el último publicista escribiera su anuncio y abandonara la sala con cara de satisfacción.

Estaba pensando cómo podía salir del conducto del aire acondicionado cuando, en la sala de al lado, los publicistas se pusieron a brindar y cantar en honor de don Pelayo y el tubo se desplomó haciéndose pedazos.

El aterrizaje no fue nada agradable, pero pronto un impulso interno me hizo olvidar el batacazo. Me acerqué a la máquina y, como PGA había dejado conectado un teclado, aproveché para escribir mis propios mensajes publicitarios.

–Ya sabéis lo que tenéis que hacer, ¿no?

–No te preocupes, este vez haremos bien nuestro trabajo –me tranquilizó mi amigo SI desde el interior del artefacto.

–Yo no pienso... hasta que... –el abuelo DO quiso protestar, pero se tuvo que callar porque nadie le hacía caso.

A la semana siguiente todo estaba preparado. Aún no habían llegado las rebajas, pero muchas tiendas disponían ya de un potente altavoz instalado en la puerta de entrada.

Para la mayoría de la gente aquél era un día normal. Con su madrugón, su desayuno a la carrera y el autobús lleno a reventar. Nadie sospechaba lo que estaba a punto de ocurrir, algo... que marcaría el rumbo de sus vidas.

A la hora convenida, una multitud de establecimientos comerciales en todo el mundo estaban preparados para emitir el anuncio que, para cada uno de ellos, les había confeccionado la Máquina de don Pelayo. Y, para cumplir todos los encargos, no había parado de trabajar ni de día ni de noche. El texto de los spots había sido redactado por los publicistas de cada ciudad, pero la música (la más sugestiva y bailable que hayáis escuchado nunca) había sido compuesta por la máquina.

Con esta música tan maravillosa, don Pelayo pretendía poseer la mente de todos los habitantes de la Tierra y arrastrarlos a comprar, durante las 24 horas del día. Para poner en marcha su plan, PGA no había ahorrado en gastos: estaba convencido de que iba a ganar montañas de dinero. Había seleccionado las voces más bellas del mundo para leer los textos de los anuncios y, para grabar las melodías, había contratado a las mejores orquestas.

Se acercaba la hora y el compositor se metió en su cama. Al verse rodeado por sus peluches favoritos, se le pasaban siempre los nervios, y ese día tenía muchos.

Los encargados de las tiendas encendieron los equipos de sonido, y los anuncios resonaron por las calles como los villancicos durante la Navidad.

Al principio nadie les hizo caso. La gente deambulaba con prisa, de aquí para allá, con el estrés habitual y sin fijarse en nada (en una flor o en la forma de una nube) que no fuera su reloj de pulsera. Pensaban en lo de siempre: cómo llegar a fin de mes, cuánto les iba a costar la factura del teléfono o desde cuándo sus hijos no les hacían caso.Y… todo era normal hasta que, sin previo aviso, su cerebro se bloqueó.

"¿Qué me está pasando?", se preguntaron todos, al mismo tiempo. "¿Por qué todo el mundo se ha parado?", "¿por qué las piernas no me responden?", "¿por qué?… ¡Eh!… ¿qué es esto que suena?... si es música, pero… ¡¡¡qué música!!!, es lo más bonito que he oído en mi vida. Un momento, esto tengo que oírlo más despacio, pero, ¿qué me pasa?, si me siento de maravilla... qué paz, qué armonía, qué energía me está entrando, sería capaz de…"

La música había atrapado sus mentes con la misma eficacia que un imán gigante. No podían escapar a su influjo invisible, porque la melodía los atraía de una manera irresistible. Sorprendidos, todos se fueron aproximando a los altavoces, sin poder hacer nada para evitarlo.

Don Pelayo daba saltos en su cama y arrancaba las piernas y los brazos de sus peluches, sin darse cuenta, de pura felicidad. Sus operarios habían instalado también cámaras en todas las tiendas que se habían apuntado a su Programa Internacional de Anuncios, y las imágenes llegaban directamente al televisor de su cuarto.

Y todavía quedaba el toque de gracia. Ahora que don Pelayo había logrado captar la atención de todo el planeta, solo tenía que transmitirles una orden, para que todos, sin excepción, la acataran, porque sus mentes estaban poseídas por la música.

–Mi pequeño Wolfy –le susurró PGA a su mascota favorita, un muñeco vestido de Mozart, que sus padres le habían regalado cuando era muy pequeño–. Ahora viene lo mejor: la música bajará de nivel y unas voces maravillosas (como las que salen en las películas) leerán los textos que los publicistas de todo el mundo han escrito en mi Máquina. Que si compre esto, que si compre lo otro, que si necesita este aparato para tener unos abdominales perfectos, que si este robot de cocina le preparará los mejores platos... ¡Qué maravilla!: ¡¡¡tengo el mundo a mis pies!!! Y gracias al poder de mi música, harán todo lo que yo les pida.

Mozart, bueno, el muñeco gastado de Mozart, lo miraba con sus ojillos inocentes, sin entender nada de nada.

–Sí, sí, amigo del alma –continuó don Pelayo con gesto paciente–, ya sé que tú también creaste una música hermosísima, capaz de poseerte por dentro y llenarte de energía, pero, querido, se te olvidó la más importante: el mensaje publicitario. Los humanos son tan tontos que siempre esperan que alguien les diga lo que tienen que hacer. Qué tienen que ponerse, qué tienen que comer, cómo han de ser sus cuerpos... Y ahora verás lo que pasa.

Y así fue. La música bajó de volumen y comenzaron a oírse los primeros mensajes publicitarios:

"LA PAZ NO ES UN DERECHO, ES UNA CONQUISTA", recitó una voz de mujer, la más sensual que haya oído nunca.

"SI TIENES PENSAMIENTOS POSITIVOS, ATRAERÁS LO POSITIVO", añadió una voz muy agradable de hombre. Y siguieron muchas más:

"ES MÁS FÁCIL REPRIMIR EL PRIMER CAPRICHO QUE SATISFACER TODOS LOS QUE LE SIGUEN", se oyó en una esquina. Y esto en otra:

"APRENDER SIN REFLEXIONAR ES MALGASTAR ENERGÍA"

"ASÍ COMO HAY UN ARTE DE HABLAR, EXISTE TAMBIÉN UN ARTE DE BIEN ESCUCHAR"

Al principio la gente miraba, desconcertada, los altavoces, porque nunca antes les habían dicho frases tan bonitas y... don Pelayo empezó a morderse los labios.

–¿Quién ha escrito eso?, ¿quién ha escrito eso? –gritaba y repetía. Gritaba y se desesperaba. Gritaba y se daba cachetes en la cara.

Pero los altavoces de todos los centros comerciales continuaban lanzando sus mensajes, totalmente ajenos a la desesperación de don Pelayo. Y muchas personas continuaban acercándose atraídas por la música y aquellas voces de ángeles.

"EL HOMBRE QUE NO SE CONTENTA CON POCO, NO SE CONTENTA CON NADA"
"PARA TENER MÁS HAY QUE DESEAR MENOS"
"¿QUÉ SENTIDO TIENE CORRER CUANDO ESTAMOS EN LA CARRETERA EQUIVOCADA?"
"EL HOMBRE HACE DINERO, PERO EL DINERO NO HACE AL HOMBRE"
"A MEDIDA QUE AVANZA UNA DISCUSIÓN, RETROCEDE LA VERDAD"
"AÑORAR EL PASADO ES CORRER TRAS EL VIENTO"
"CAER ESTÁ PERMITIDO. ¡LEVANTARSE ES OBLIGATORIO!"
"DISFRUTA HOY, ES MÁS TARDE DE LO QUE CREES"
"COMO NO SABÍAN QUE ERA IMPOSIBLE, LO HICIERON"

Don Pelayo bajó de la cama y, con la boca llena de espuma y los ojos fuera de sus órbitas, marcó un número en su teléfono móvil.

–¡Paren todo esto!, ¡apaguen los equipos de megafonía! –ordenaba a diestro y siniestro.

Cuando, de tanto gritar, se quedó afónico, se dio cuenta de que el teléfono no funcionaba. Alguien le había quitado la batería. Salió de su cuarto dispuesto a atrapar al responsable (o responsables) de todo aquello, pero la música que llegaba desde la calle había atraído también a sus guardias de seguridad, con porra y todo, y

STOP
30,€

estaba completamente solo en la casa. Y como su nueva mansión era realmente grande, tardó bastante tiempo en poder salir de allí.

–Recuérdame que, cuando se solucione todo esto –le comunicó a su muñeco de Mozart que seguía llevando en la mano, aunque lo había llenado todo de babas verdes–, no vuelva a comprar una casa con tantas puertas y tantos cuartos de baño.

El aire fresco de la mañana le golpeó en la nariz nada más pisar la calle.

–¡Policía, policía! ¡Me han estafado, me han estafado!

Por más que corría y resoplaba con el esfuerzo, no encontró a nadie. Dobló esquinas con bares y tiendas, atravesó pasadizos repletos de locales comerciales, recorrió las galerías de los mercados, pero allí no encontró ni un alma. Todo estaba vacío. Las cosas materiales seguían allí, con sus precios y sus etiquetas, pero no había nadie comprando, ni tampoco... vendiendo.

–¿Es que el mundo se ha vuelto loco? –dio un grito sobrehumano y se precipitó al suelo llorando como un niño al que le hubieran quitado de las manos un enorme pastel de nata y fresa.

Arrastrándose por la acera al más puro estilo de los reptiles, PGA se aproximó a un escaparate lleno de televisores y, entonces, solo entonces, lo comprendió todo.

–*Señoras y señores* –decía el locutor de la televisión con cara de espanto–, *abrimos este informativo de urgencia, con una noticia de última hora. La Guerra de Irak ha terminado. Sí, han oído bien. Y no solo eso, nos están llegando unas imágenes realmente asombrosas desde la zona de los combates: los soldados de los dos bandos han arrojado sus fusiles y ametralladoras al suelo y se están.... se están... ¡¡¡ abrazando!!!*

Al presentador se le escaparon varias lágrimas, una cosa que tenían completamente prohibida.

–*Señores telespectadores* –logró continuar a duras penas–, *llevo 40 años en esto del periodismo y nunca había visto nada igual.*

—¡Interrumpimos la programación habitual, para ofrecerles un avance informativo! —se oía desde otra pantalla que sintonizaba otra cadena—. *El precio del petróleo está bajando a un ritmo histórico, y es que ningún hombre de negocios quiere comprar ni un litro más del que le hace falta a su compañía y, como sobra, el precio del barril está cayendo en picado. Y esto no es todo, conectamos con nuestro corresponsal en la bolsa de Nueva York, porque allí también está pasando algo muy, pero que muy raro. Adelante, Filiberto.*

—Buenos días, desde Estados Unidos. ¡No os lo vais a creer! Los representantes de las compañías multinacionales están regalando miles de sacos de trigo y arroz a los pueblos más pobres del planeta. Además, nos dicen que ellos, personalmente, llevarán la comida a sus hermanos del sur y que ya se ha acabado eso de pasar hambre, mientras las personas de los países ricos se mueren de tan gordos como están.

—Filiberto, ¿has tomado hoy vino para desayunar?

—No, compañeros de los estudios centrales, estoy fresco como una rosa. Es más, nunca me había sentido tan bien, con tanta energía, no sé si en el viejo continente ha pasado lo mismo que aquí. Una especie de música maravillosa nos ha despertado a todos y, al oírla, a la gente le ha dado por hacer cosas muy raras.

—Gracias, Filiberto y tenemos que cerrar la conexión con la bolsa de Nueva York, porque nos pide paso urgente nuestro enviado especial a Tokio.

—Buenas noches desde Asia. Les habla Antonio Cansino. Las principales empresas del sector electrónico han parado sus cadenas de producción. Los operarios nos dicen que ya hay bastantes aparatos electrónicos en el mundo —como televisores, videoconsolas y cosas así— y que ahora lo que interesa es que la gente salga a los parques y juegue con sus hijos y haga ejercicio o descanse sentada debajo de un árbol.

—¡Vivir para ver! Gracias, esta ha sido nuestra conexión de urgencia desde Japón. Pero no paran de llegarnos noticias urgentes desde los cinco continentes. Les leo algunas:

Rusia. "Pasa mi abrazo". Con este lema, centenares de moscovitas se han reunido en la Plaza del Kremlin y no paran de darse abrazos. Esta inusual concentración se está repitiendo en todas las ciudades rusas y en ellas participan ciudadanos de todas las etnias.

Kenia. Los cazadores furtivos han dejado de disparar a los elefantes para sacarles el marfil de sus colmillos. Parece ser que las fábricas han decidido hacer ahora las figuras decorativas con mármol, en vez de marfil, para no matar a estos animales tan hermosos.

Italia. Ciudadanos de todo tipo están vendiendo joyas y otros objetos de valor. Aseguran que ya tienen bastante y que invertirán el dinero que les den en proyectos de cooperación en África y América Latina.

España. Padres y madres trabajadoras han acudido en masa a las guarderías para estar con sus hijos. Muchos empresarios han dado el día libre a sus empleados y les han comunicado que, a partir de ahora, no hace falta que trabajen tantas horas.

Don Pelayo volvió a su mansión arrastrando los pies. Su sueño de convertirse en el hombre más rico de la Tierra se acababa de esfumar.

El resto es fácil de contar. A don Pelayo le esperaba en la azotea de su mansión un vehículo volador que lanzaba luces centelleantes y que se lo llevó a toda prisa. ¿Veis como era un extraterrestre y que los suyos vinieron a rescatarlo después de su sonado –y nunca mejor dicho– fracaso? Espero que los habitantes de otros planetas no sean tan vengativos como los de la Tierra, porque si no…

Cuando el OVNI (o ¿era un helicóptero de la policía?) desapareció por el cielo, yo pude salir de mi escondrijo y me puse a buscar la Máquina Musical de los Deseos, pero, por más que busqué y busqué, fui incapaz de encontrarla.

¿Dónde habrían ido mis amigos, los sonidos musicales? Casi me echo a llorar. De pronto me sentía terriblemente sola. Sin el abuelo DO (siempre quejándose), sin la abuela RE (con sus cuentos fantásticos), sin la energía de mi amigo SI… Sentía, por primera vez, que me faltaba algo, algo muy importante, hasta que….

Me soné los mocos y llegó a mi oído el sutil canto de un pajarillo. Me gustó tanto que decidí abrir mis orejas de par en par (maniobra que creo no haber hecho nunca antes) y…¡qué emoción!... capté el aleteo de las golondrinas, el susurro de las copas de los árboles, el gorgoteo de una fuente.

Después, allá a lo lejos, distinguí las notas de un piano y, mucho más cerca de mí, una radio me inundó con una balada de rock. Y entonces me entraron unas ganas enormes de reír. Mis amigos no me habían abandonado, sino que seguían ahí, a mi alrededor, jugando al escondite, porque los sonidos son sonidos y no se pueden ver, pero los sientes, porque siempre están con nosotros y nos acompañan en los momentos buenos, y también en los malos, cuando, por ejemplo, se desata una tormenta y los relámpagos te taponan las oídos.

Solo hay que limpiarse bien las orejas y… aprender a escuchar, porque los sonidos tienen aún muchas cosas maravillosas que contarnos.